The Art of City-Making

Charles Landry

EARTHSCAN

London • Sterling, VA

First published by Earthscan in the UK and USA in 2006

Copyright © Charles Landry, 2006

ISBN-10:   1-84407-245-2 paperback
           1-84407-246-0 hardback
ISBN-13:   978-1-84407-245-3 paperback
           978-1-84407-246-0 hardback

Typeset by MapSet Ltd, Gateshead, UK
Printed and bound in the UK by Cromwell Press, Trowbridge, UK
Cover design by Susanne Harris

For a full list of publications please contact:

Earthscan
8–12 Camden High Street
London, NW1 0JH, UK
Tel: +44 (0)20 7387 8558
Fax: +44 (0)20 7387 8998
Email: earthinfo@earthscan.co.uk
Web: www.earthscan.co.uk

22883 Quicksilver Drive, Sterling, VA 20166-2012, USA

Earthscan is an imprint of James and James (Science Publishers) Ltd and
publishes in association with the International Institute for Environment
and Development

A catalogue record for this book is available from the British Library

Library of Congress Cataloging-in-Publication Data

Landry, Charles.
  The art of city-making / Charles Landry.
    p. cm.
  ISBN-13: 978-1-84407-245-3 (pbk.)
  ISBN-10: 1-84407-245-2 (pbk.)
  ISBN-13: 978-1-84407-246-0 (hardback)
  ISBN-10: 1-84407-246-0 (hardback)
  1. City planning. 2. City and town life. I. Title.
  HT166.L329 2006
  307.1'216—dc22

                                          2006021878

The paper used for this book is FSC-certified and
totally chlorine-free. FSC (the Forest Stewardship
Council) is an international network to promote
responsible management of the world's forests.

Mixed Sources
Product group from well-managed
forests and other controlled sources
www.fsc.org Cert no. TT-TOC-2082
© 1996 Forest Stewardship Council

Contents

List of Boxes

List of Photographs

Sources are credited beside each photograph for those in the list below. All photographs in the two colour sections are by Charles Landry.

Acronyms and Abbreviations

3PL	third party logistics
BID	business improvement district
BME	black and minority ethnic
CABE	Commission on Architecture and the Built Environment
CDM	Construction, Design and Management
CIAM	Congres Internationaux d'Architecture Moderne
CLES	Centre for Local Economic Strategy
CNU	Congress of New Urbanism
GaWC	Global and World Cities
IBA	International Bauaustellung
ICLEI	International Council for Local Environmental Initiatives
IPPUC	Institute of Urban Planning and Research of Curitiba
IR	integrated resort
KVI	known value item
MACBA	Museum of Modern Art of Barcelona
MFP	Multifunction Polis
NPF	National Planning Forum
PPS	Planning Policy Statement
RFID	radio frequency identification
TEU	twenty foot equivalent unit
UDA	Urban Design Alliance
UNESCO	United Nations Educational, Scientific and Cultural Organization

Acknowledgements

Writing a book is never a lone endeavour. You learn from others, you pick up ideas, someone gives you a crisp turn of phrase that encapsulates a point well. Someone encourages you and gives you confidence. I have many people to thank: Ed Beerbohm, who helped craft the text into a sharper form and did the research for the section 'The City as a Guzzling Beast'; Gabrielle Boyle, for the conversations; Jim Bage; and then the many people I have worked with, especially Margie Caust and Richard Brecknock, who put my Adelaide Thinkers in Residence programme together; and Mike Rann, the Premier of South Australia who appointed me as 'thinker'. The Adelaide period in 2003 gave me a real chance to think some things through and the chapter 'The City as a Living Work of Art' comes from that period. John Worthington of DEGW and chair of Building Futures gave me the opportunity to write *Riding the Rapids: Urban Life in an Age of Complexity*, and the 'Unscrambling Complexity' sections benefited from that collaboration. Honor Chapman (formerly of Future London) and Greg Clark provided the chance to research the background to the sections on 'Aligning Professional Mindsets' and 'Blindspots in City-Making'. Chris Murray commissioned work on creativity and risk, which is a theme throughout the book. My Swiss friends Toni Linder, Petra Bischoff and Elisa Fuchs gave me the chance to try out ideas in the book in Albania and the opportunity to survey projects throughout southeastern Europe, from Ukraine to Bosnia. This has appeared as *Culture at the Heart of Transformation*. Besim Petrela managed many trips throughout Albania and his surgeon brother operated on my septic arm in the middle of the night in Tirana. Carol Coletta from Smart Cities is a friend but also asked me write a series of letters called 'Letters to Urban Leaders' to the CEOs for Cities network in the States, of which she is director. Key ideas from those appear throughout the text. Others who need thanking include: Phil Wood and Jude Bloomfield, especially in relation to the Intercultural City project; Marc Pachter; Meg van Rosendaal; Simon Brault; Jonathan Hyams; Nick Falk; Dickon Robinson; Peter Kageyama; Andy Howell; Masayuki Sasaki; my friends from Metaa in Korea; Paul Brown; Thierry Baert; Christine Sullivan; Patricia Zaido; Erin Williams; Evert Verhagen; Susan Serran; Tim Jones; Doug Pigg; Theresa McDonagh; Richard Best; Richard Jackson; Martin Evans; Andrew Kelly; Hamish Ironside from Earthscan; Robert Palmer; Leonie Sandercock ... and of course the growing family of wild ducks outside my window, which are a good source of distraction.

1

Overture

City-making is a complex art; it is not a formula. There is no simplistic, ten-point plan that can be mechanically applied to guarantee success in any eventuality.

But there are some strong principles that can help send good city-making on its way:

- The most significant argument of *The Art of City-Making* is that a city should not seek to be the most creative city *in* the world (or region or state) – it should strive to be the best and most imaginative city *for* the world.[1] This one change of word – from 'in' to 'for' – has dramatic implications for a city's operating dynamics. It gives city-making an *ethical* foundation. It helps the aim of cities becoming *places of solidarity*, where the relations of the individual, the group and the outsider to the city and the planet are in better alignment. These can be cities of passion and compassion.
- Go with the grain of local cultures and their distinctiveness, yet be open to outside influences. Balance local and global.
- Involve those affected by what you do in decision-making. It is astonishing how ordinary people can make the extraordinary happen, given the chance.
- Learn from what others have done well, but don't copy them thoughtlessly. Cities focused mainly on best practices are followers not leaders and do not take the required risks to move themselves forward.
- Encourage projects that add value economically while simultaneously reinforcing ethical values. This means revisiting the

balance between individual wants and collective and planetary needs relevant to the 21st century. Too often value is defined narrowly in terms of financial calculus. This is naïve. The new economy requires an ethical value base to guide action. It will imply behaviour change to meet value-based goals such as putting a halt to the exploitation of the environment. Combining social and environmental with economic account-ing helps identify projects that pass this test. The 'fair trade' movement is an example.

- Every place can make more out of its potential if the precondi-tions to think, plan and act with imagination are present. The imagination of people, combined with other qualities such as tenacity and courage, is our greatest resource.
- Foster *civic creativity* as the ethos of your city. Civic creativity is imaginative problem-solving applied to public good objec-tives. It involves the public sector being more entrepreneurial, though within the bounds of accountability, and the private sector being more aware of its responsibilities to the collective whole.

You will come across recurring themes in *The Art of City-Making*. These include the following:

- Our sensory landscape is shrinking precisely at the moment when it should be broadening. Sensory manipulation is distanc-ing us from our cities and we are losing our visceral knowledge of them. We have forgotten how to understand the smells of the city, to listen to its noises, to grasp the messages its look sends out and to be aware of its materials. Instead there is infor-mation and sensory overload in the name of making the city a spectacular experience.
- The city is discussed in barren, eviscerated terms and in techni-cal jargon by urban professionals as it if were a lifeless, detached being. In fact, it is a sensory, emotional, lived *experi-ence*. Cities are like relatives: you never really escape. The city is more than hardware. How often do strategic urban plans start with the words 'beauty', 'love', 'happiness' or 'excite-ment', as opposed to 'bypass', 'spatial outcome' or 'planning framework'?
- To understand the city and to capture its potential requires us to deal with five major blindspots: we need to *think* differently

– in a more rounded way – in order to see the connections between things; we need to *perceive* the city as a more comprehensively sensory experience, so understanding its effect on individuals; we need to *feel* the city as an emotional experience; we need to *understand* cities culturally – cultural literacy is the skill that will help us better understand the dynamics of cities; and we need to *recognize the artistic* in all of us, which can lead us to a different level of experience.

- An understanding of culture, in contrast to economics or sociology, is a superior way of describing the world because it can explain change and its causes and effects and does not take any ideology, institution or practice for granted or treat them as immutable. Culture is concerned with human behaviours and so cultural analysis can be expressed in human terms we find familiar and engaging. It is thus a good medium through which to provide stories about the world.

- Cities need stories or cultural narratives about themselves to both anchor and drive identity as well as to galvanize citizens. These stories allow individuals to submerge themselves into bigger, more lofty endeavours. A city which describes itself as the 'city of churches' fosters different behavioural patterns in citizens than a city that projects itself as a 'city of second chances'. (Critics complain, however, that such cultural narratives are difficult to measure. We shall return to this contention later.)

- The internal logic of the unfettered market reveals a limited story of ambition and no ethics or morality. It has no view of the 'good life', of social mixing, of mutual caring or nurturing the environment. There is an imperative to make the market system *serve* the bigger picture – through incentives, regulations … or whatever. This places responsibility on *us*.

- Like a veil, the market system shrouds our consciousness while plumping up desire and consumption. The market logic has a tendency to fragment groups into units of consumption and enclaves and, in so doing, to break up social solidarities. But the latter are needed if intractable urban problems such as meeting responsibility for the public realm or natural surveillance are to be achieved.

A conceptual framework is offered to help us unscramble complexity. It focuses on assessing deeper faultlines and problems that will

Creative city-making is a fragile affair, requiring constant alertness within an ethical framework of values

Source: Collin Bogaars

take generations to solve: traditional drivers such as IT and the ageing population; battlegrounds and the day-to-day contests over priorities; and paradoxes such as the simultaneous rise of a risk-averse culture with a pressure to be creative and to break the rules.

Some of the main points made in *The Art of City-Making* are that the overall dynamic of the system that governs city-making is far less rational than it makes itself appear – it does not look at comprehensive flows, connections or inter-relationships, and down-stream impacts are not seen or costed; that city-making is no one's job – the urban professions and politicians may believe it is theirs, but they are only responsible for a part; that because of this frag-mentation and the competing rules of different professions and interests we cannot build the cities we love anymore – the current rules, especially concerning traffic engineering, forbid it. And, not least, that 6 billion people on the planet is too many unless lifestyles change dramatically.

The Art of City-Making proposes that we:

- Redefine the scope of creativity, focusing much more on unleashing the mass of ordinary, day-to-day, dormant creativity that lies within most of us. The focus should fall equally on social and other forms of creativity. This would represent a shift in attention from assuming creativity only comprises the creative industries and media. Creativity is in danger of being swallowed up by fashion.
- Recognize artistic thinking as helpful in finding imaginative solutions and engaging and moving people. All urban profes-sions should consider thinking like artists, planning like generals and acting like impresarios.
- Rethink who our celebrities are and what an urban heroine or hero should be. This could be an invisible planner, a business person, a social worker or an artist.

- See that there is a major opportunity for the return of the city state and for cities to become value-driven to a much greater extent than nation states can ever be. This entails renegotiating power relations with national governments.

At its best, good city-making leads to the highest achievement of human culture. A cursory look at the globe reveals the names of cities old and new. Their names resonate as we think simultaneously about their physical presence, their activities, their cultures, and their people and ideas: Cairo, Isfahan, Delhi, Rome, Constantinople, Canton/Gúangzhōu, Kyoto, New York, San Francisco, Shanghai, Vancouver, or, on a smaller scale, Berne, Florence, Varanasi, Shibam. Our best cities are the most elaborate and sophisticated artefacts humans have conceived, shaped and made. The worst are forgettable, damaging, destructive, even hellish. For too long we believed that city-making involved only the art of architecture and land-use planning. Over time, the arts of engineering, surveying, valuing, property development and project management began to form part of the pantheon. We now know that the art of city-making involves all the arts; the physical alone do not make a city or a place. For that to happen, the art of understanding human needs, wants and desires; the art of generating wealth and bending the dynamics of the market and economics to the city's needs; the art of circulation and city movement; the art of urban design; and the art of trading power for creative influence so the power of people is unleashed must all be deployed. We could go on. And let's not forget community endorsement, health, inspiration and celebration. Most importantly, good city-making requires the art of adding value and values simultaneously in everything undertaken. Together, the mindsets, skills and values embodied in these arts help make places out of simple spaces.

The city is an interconnected whole. It cannot be viewed as merely a series of elements, although each element is important in its own right. When we consider a constituent part we cannot ignore its relation to the rest. The building speaks to its neighbouring building and to the street, and the street in turn helps fashion its neighbourhood. Infused throughout are the people who populate the city. They mould the physical into shape and frame its use and how it feels.

The city comprises both hard and soft infrastructure. The hard is like the bone structure, the skeleton, while the soft is akin to the nervous system and its synapses. One cannot exist without the other.

The city is a multifaceted entity. It is an economic structure – an economy; it is a community of people – a society; it is a designed environment – an artefact; and it is a natural environment – an ecosystem. And it is all four of these – economy, society, artefact and ecosystem – governed by an agreed set of rules – a polity. Its inner engine or animating force, however, is its culture. Culture – the things we find important, beliefs and habits – gives the city its distinctiveness – its flavour, tone and patina. The art of city-making touches all these dimensions. City-making is about choices, and therefore about politics, and therefore about the play of power. And our cities reflect the forces of power that have shaped them.

The Art of City-Making is quite a long book, but there are different rhythms beating in its pages and I hope it is easy to read in bite-sized, self-contained chunks. For instance, Chapter 2 ('The Sensory Landscape of Cities') has one mood and attempts to be lyrical in parts, while the section on 'The City as a Guzzling Beast' (Chapter 3) is fact-driven, and the sections on the geography of misery and desire have a more exasperated tone. The second half of the book seeks to bring all these things together, to clarify and simplify, and to help the reader throw light on complex, bigger issues affecting cities. Thus, as we draw towards the end, Chapter 6 ('The City as a Living Work of Art') is like a toolbox of ideas with which to move forward. And 'Creative Cities for the World' and 'Creativity and the City: Thinking Through the Steps' invite the reader to make their own judgements about what places are really inventive and why.

City-making and responsibility

Whose responsibility is it to make our cities? While the forms they take are usually unintentional, cities are not mere accidents. They are the product of decisions made for individual, separate, even disparate purposes, whose inter-relationships and side-effects have not been fully considered.

City-making is in fact no one person's job. Politicians say it is theirs, but they can get too concerned with managing a party rather than a city. Elected officials can get addicted to shorter-term thinking. The imperative to get re-elected can stifle leadership, risks are not taken, and easy wins or instantly visible results – the building

of a bypass, say, or putting up as many housing units as possible –
are thrust to the fore. Perhaps a local partnership or a chief execu-
tive officer is responsible? No – probably not.

The urban professions would claim they are in charge, even
though they are responsible only for aspects of the physical parts.
Yet if there is no conscious overarching sense of city- or place-
making, we go by default patterns and the core assumptions of each
profession – their technical codes, standards and guidelines, such as
those that set patterns for a turning circle or the width of pavements. But such codes, standards and guidelines do not, on their
own, provide a cohesive template for city-making. The technical
knowledge of highway engineers, surveyors, planners or architects,
viewed in isolation, is probably fine, albeit requiring rethinking on
occasion, but a technical manual does not create a bigger picture of
what a city is, where it could be going and how it fits into a global
pattern.

It is no one person's job at present to connect the agendas, ways
of thinking, knowledge and skill bases. But if, at present, no one is
responsible, then everyone is to blame for our many ugly, soulless,
unworkable cities and our occasional places of delight. And there is
a pass-the-parcel attitude to responsibility. One moment the
highway engineers are the scapegoats, the next it's the planner or
the developer. What is needed is more than being a mere networker
or broker of professions and requires a deeply etched understanding of what essence each professional grouping brings or could
bring to the art of city-making.

The spirit of city-making, with its necessary creativity and
imagination, is more like improvised jazz than chamber music.
There is experimentation, trial and error, and everyone can be a
leader, given a particular area of expertise. As if by some mysteri-
ous process, orchestration occurs through seemingly unwritten
rules. Good city-making requires myriad acts of persistence and
courage that need to be aligned like a good piece of music. There is
not just one conductor, which is why leadership in its fullest sense
is so important – seemingly disparate parts have to be melded into
a whole.

Art and science

The Art of City-Making privileges the word 'art' over 'science'. It
acknowledges, though, that we can still be scientific in the proce-

dures of how we approach city issues. As in the natural sciences, we can define questions, gather information and resources, form hypotheses, analyse facts and data and on occasion perform experiments, and certainly interpret things and draw conclusions that serve as a starting point for new hypotheses. But given the array of things in a city to consider, different forms of insight are needed, and these change all the time, for example from the hard science of engineering to the soft science of environmental psychology. Adhering to methodologies is inappropriate. Science assumes a predictability that the human ecologies that are cities cannot provide.

The phrase 'the art of' in itself implies judgements of value. We are in the realm of the subjective. It implies there is a profound understanding of each city-making area, but also, in addition, the ability to grasp the essence of other subjects, to be *interdisciplinary*. The methods used to gain insight and knowledge are broadranging, from simple listening to more formalized comparative methods and understanding how intangible issues like image can help urban competitiveness. These arts are in fact skills acquired by experience and acute observation, requiring deep knowledge, the use of imagination and discipline.

Fine judgement is key to city-making. What works in one situation, even when the factors seem the same, may not work in another. For example, to launch the long-term image and self-perception campaign in Leicester, posters declaring 'Leicester is boring' worked positively because there was enough resilience in the city to both understand the nuggets of truth embodied in the campaign and to respond actively to the criticism and to appreciate irony. The steering groups involved decided prior to the campaign that this was an appropriate approach for Leicester. However, a similar, 'negative' approach in neighbouring Derby, for example, may have been deemed culturally insensitive, ineffectual or just plain unsuitable. Knowledge of local cultural particularities and context is therefore always paramount. But while specialized judgement in particular cases is key, there are also principles that tend to work across particularities, such as going with, rather than against, the grain of peoples' cultural backgrounds in implementing projects.

The compound *city-making* is preferred to *city-building*, since the latter implies that the city is only that which the built environment professions have physically constructed. Yet what gives

a city life, meaning and purpose are the *acts* people perform on
the physical stage. The stage set is not the play. The physical
things are only the accoutrements, helpful instruments and
devices. But the aim here is to shift the balance, to increase the
credibility and status of the scriptwriters, the directors and
performers. Countless skills come to mind. The core professions,
beyond the built environment people, include environmental and
social occupations such as conservation advisers or care professionals, economic development specialists, the IT community,
community professions and volunteers, and 'cross-cutting' people
such as urban regeneration experts. There are also historians,
anthropologists, people who understand popular culture, geogra-
phers, psychologists and many other specialists. And there is a
still wider group – including educators, the police, health workers,
local businesses and the media – that makes a city tick. Then there
is the wider public itself, the glue that ties things together. Within
all these groups, there is a need for visionaries who can pinpoint
what each city's prospects are and where it might be going. Unless
all these people are part of the urban story, the physical remains
an empty shell.

Yet too often we rely on the priesthood of those concerned with
the physical, and it is they, perhaps more than others, who are
responsible for the cities we have. Acerbically we might ask: Do
they understand people and their emotions? Do some of them even
like people?

Push and pull

Transitional periods of history, like the Industrial Revolution or the
technological revolution of the past 50 years, can produce confusion – a sense of liberation combined with a feeling of being swept
along by events. It thus takes a while for new ethical stances to take
root or to establish new and coherent worldviews. For example,
the link between the individual and the group is gradually being
reconfigured, as bonds to traditional place-based communities have
fractured and been weakened by increasing mobility and decreas-
ing provision by public authorities. Creating stable, local identities
or senses of belonging in this context is difficult.

The temper of the age is one of uncertainty, foreboding, vulner-
ability and lack of control over overweening global forces. It is hard
to see a way to a Golden Age. Among the present-day young, the

Zeitgeist of the 1960s generation, with its sense of 'we can change the world', is absent. A significant proportion of the young today feel change is potentially threatening rather than liberating. But what is different about the spirit of the age is the recognition that the long-term effects of industrialism have hidden real costs.

City mayors or key officials know about the contradictory demands of successful city-making in this context. They experience and navigate the push and pull of clearing rubbish, reducing noise, curtailing crime, making movement and transport easy, ensuring urban services, housing and health facilities are up to speed, while leaving something in the kitty for culture. Day-to-day life needs to work.

But mayors and their cities have to paint on a much larger canvas if they are to generate the wealth and prosperity to fund the necessary investments in infrastructures and facilities that generate the quality of life of their cities.

Cities must speak to a world well beyond national government. They need to attract investment bankers, inward-investing companies, property developers, the talented the world over. They need to court the media through which the city's resonance is either confirmed or generated.

To survive well, bigger cities must play on varied stages – from the immediately local, through the regional and national, to the widest global platform. These mixed targets, goals and audiences each demand something different. Often they pull and stretch in diverging directions. How do you create coherence out of wants and needs that do not align?

One demands a local bus stop shelter, another airport connectivity across the world; one audience wants just a few tourists to ensure the city remains more distinctly itself, another as many as possible to generate money; one wants to encourage local business incubators, another a global brand; for some, an instantly recognizable city brand to disseminate is the way forward, for others it is merely copying the crowd. The list is endless.

Working on different scales and complexity is hard: the challenge is to coalesce, align and unify this diversity so the resulting city feels coherent and can operate consistently.

But lurking in the background are bigger issues that play on the mind of the more visionary urban leader, issues that the world cannot avoid and that cities have to respond to. Global sustainability is one. And this is a consideration that should shape what cities do, how we build, how we move about, how we behave and how we avert pollution. Taken seriously, it requires dramatic behavioural change, since technological solutions can only take us so far.

There is already an air of resignation, tinged with guilt, in individuals and decision-makers alike; we cannot face the implications of getting out of the car or refitting the economy for the period beyond the oil age. But that time is coming at us fast. It is too easy to respond only when the horse has already bolted. It is too difficult, too many feel, to argue for the switch to public transport, to generate the taxes to create a transport system that feels great to use as much for the well-off as for those at the other end of the scale. This means rethinking density and sprawl. But everyone knows the economic equations and urban formations that make this work as well as the tricks that seduce the user: city regions with hubs and nodes, incentives like park and ride, and disincentives to travel by car.

The issue has been solved in many parts of the world – think of Hong Kong or Curitiba – but it requires a different view of public investment and investment in the public good and, essentially, depends on how much the individual is prepared to give up for wider public purposes.

As already mentioned, there is a tendency to pass the parcel on responsibility. Some say it should be government taking the lead, but at the same time these people do not want government to be so powerful. Yet many US cities have taken the lead over national government and signed the Kyoto agreement, for example, reminding us of the power of cities to drive national agendas.

But sustainability addresses more than environmental concerns. It has at least four pillars: the economic, social, cultural and ecological. And there is more to add. Cities need to be emotionally and psychologically sustaining, and issues like the quality and design of the built environment, the quality of connections between people and the organizational capacity of urban stakeholders become crucial, as do issues of spatial segregation in cities and poverty. Sustainable places need to be sustaining across the range.

Unresolved and unclear

There are many opinions in the text that follows and various conclusions are reached about how cities should move forward. Where do these judgements come from, what is their basis and what is the evidence?[2] What I have laid out comes from my experience of observing cities; from participating in projects in cities from the small to the large; from talking to city leaders and the more powerful about how they want to make their cities better; and from talking to activists and the less powerful about what they want to change and how they are going to do it.

This has made me even more curious about cities – I want to know how they work and how and why they succeed or fail. I have reflected on these encounters and am left with many unanswered questions. As an example, I keep on thinking of the balances that need to be achieved and then worry that this leads to compromise and blandness: creating urban delights or curtailing urban misery; focusing on density or being lax with sprawl; worrying about what the world thinks of your city or just getting on with it regardless. Alternatively I have been thinking of questions like: Is it possible to create places where people from different backgrounds intermingle and where segregation is reduced? How can you tap the dormant energy of people that coexists side by side with pervasive passivity? What skills, talents, insight and knowledge are needed to make cities work? What qualities are needed to be a good city-maker? Imagination, for sure, but what about courage, commitment and cleverness? Is it worth having lofty aims about cities and does this provide the motivation, energy and will to change things?

My intention is to start a conversation with whoever is reading this as if we were mutually critical friends. Because of that I have tried to write in a conversational style. I know many academics will find this irritating. Yet I have a reader in mind who is probably responsible for some field of city-making, someone who is somewhat ground down by the difficulties of getting things done, who has high-flown ideals, who wants to be active yet feels they should stand back and contemplate, but who does not want to engage with a weighty tome. I have tried to switch between the evocative, the conceptual, the anecdotal and the exemplary and I hope this rhythm works. This is not a step-by-step guide. It is an exploration that proposes we think of cities in enriched ways and in which I try to highlight things I think are important yet hidden.

Secular humanism

A final point: *The Art of City-Making* is laden with assumptions that shape what I say, the suggestions I make and the preferences I have. These will probably become clear to you as the text unfolds. Nevertheless, since cities are such contested fields, both in terms of their actual functioning and what is said about them, I feel it is right to make my ideological position explicit from the outset.

I subscribe to a secular humanist position that privileges civic values, which in essence seek to foster competent, confident and engaged citizenship. Mine is an attitude or philosophy concerned with the capabilities, interests and achievements of human beings rather than the concepts and problems of science or theology. It does not decry the virtues of science or the sustenance religion or other belief systems give. It is simply that its focus is on how people live together. The world is best understood, I posit, by reasoning and conversation without reference to higher authorities. It claims life can be best lived by applying ethics; which are an attempt to arrive at practical standards that provide principles to guide our common views and behaviour and to help resolve conflicts. It provides a frame within which difference can be lived and shared with mutual respect.

Secular humanism as a core Enlightenment project has been drained of confidence. It feels exhausted and consequently is mistakenly accused of being 'wishy-washy', with no apparent point of view. Its confidence needs to be restored. The confident secular humanist view proposes a set of civic values and rules of engage-ment which include providing settings for a continually renewing dialogue across differences, cultures and conflicts; allowing strongly held beliefs or faiths expression within this core agreement; and acknowledging the 'naturalness' of conflict and establishing means and mediation devices to deal with difference. It seeks to consoli-date different ways of living, recognizing arenas in which we must all live together and those where we can live apart. It generates structured opportunities to learn to know 'the other', to explore and discover similarity and difference. It wishes to drive down decision-making on the subsidiarity principle, which implies much greater decentralization and devolution of power. Central govern-ment takes on a more subsidiary role. This enhances participation and connectivity at local level. It helps generate interest, concern and responsibility.

'Secular' does not mean emotionally barren. In fact I treasure the heightened registers of being that spirituality evokes. Indeed its animating force may be just the thing that makes some cities more liveable in than others.

Shifting the Zeitgeist

Better choices, politics and power

City-making is about making choices, applying values, using politics to turn values into policies and exerting power to get your way. Choices reflect our beliefs and attitudes, which are based on values and value judgements. These in turn are shaped by our culture. So the scope, possibilities, style and tenor of a city's physical look and its social, ecological and economic development are culturally shaped – culture moves centre-stage. If, for example, a culture invests its faith only in the market principle and trusts the drive of capital to produce sensible choices, the logic, interests and points of view of those who control markets will count for more than those who believe market-based decision-making is an essentially impoverished system of choosing.[3] If a culture holds that individual choice is everything – individuals always know best – this impacts the city. Conversely, if it is held that there is something in the idea of a public, common or collective good that has value and is beyond the vagaries of the market, credence can be given to inspirational and emblematic projects that can lift the public spirit: buildings that are not constructed according to market principles, imitate environmental initiatives, attending to the sickly or investing in youth.

City-making is a cultural project involving a battle about power. Power determines the kind of cities we have and politics is its medium. What are the effects of these different values? Consider Mercer's 'quality of living' rankings of 2006.[4] This US company's annual survey of 350 cities, focused especially on expatriates, is now seen as authoritative. It considers 39 criteria covering economics, politics, safety, housing and lifestyle. European, Canadian and Australian cities dominate the rankings, with Zurich, Geneva and Vancouver the top three, followed by Vienna. Six of the top eight cities are European. The implications of the market-driven US approach for how city life actual feels to individuals is instructive. The top US cities are Honolulu at 27th and San Francisco at 28th; Houston, where you cannot walk the streets even if you want to, is the worst of all large US cities at 68th.

Challenging the paradigm

The Art of City-Making wants to be a butterfly whose small movements contribute with many others to grander effects on a global scale. It feels to me that the Zeitgeist is ready to shift, and I want this book to be part of encouraging a new spirit of the times. This involves more than just altering the climate of opinion or intellectual atmosphere. A Zeitgeist is felt more deeply. It is less malleable and it is sensed viscerally, so providing energy and focus. It makes every person who feels it want to be an active agent, pulling them along with a comforting and comfortable instinct bordering on faith.

In each period of history we can discern overarching qualities; these are never formulaic and often contradictory. Intellectual, political, economic and social trends are etched with the characteristic spirit of their era. We can say 'modern times' are characterized by an unwavering belief in a particular, progressive view of science on its inexorable journey to the truth, and a faith in technology. Yet the 'rationality' of technology is being called into question and critiques of this approach are escalating in number. (As an example, what is rational about creating global warming and its consequences?) Post-modernism rejects the grand unifying narratives associated with the modern period that try to explain everything. The relative, multiple, culturally determined truths it upholds destabilize the position of the many who want a single answer, so unsurprisingly the truths of the Gods are back. They provide certainty and anchoring. But both the modern and the post-modern exacerbate the fragmentation of knowledge, the one through specialized research and scientific data and the other through the diversity of perspectives. The Enlightenment ideals of progress and reason have taken a battering; their confidence has been shaken.

The ethical anchor

What is the quality of the Zeitgeist seeking to emerge? At its core is a belief in thinking in a rounded way and seeing different perspectives, not putting things in separate boxes. Thinking differently also means doing things differently and sometimes means doing different things. In the struggle about what is important, those pushing this Zeitgeist seek some form of unity beyond the ding-dong of either/or arguments.[5] They believe in 'seeing the wood and the trees simultaneously', with 'strategy and tactics as one'. They are able to 'operate both with the market and against the market' and to 'assess things in terms of the precautionary principle and take risks at the same time' or 'to go with the flow of ambiguity but still be clear about where you are going'. This allows them to see things in more depth. They work against compartmentalized, 'silo' thinking and the turgid bureaucracy of departmental baronies. They are against reductionism, which thinks about parts in isolation and sees the city in its parts, and instead consider the interconnected, overall dynamics, such as how socio-economic exigencies and crime inextricably interconnect. It is difficult, if not impossible, to understand wholes by focusing on the parts, yet it is possible to understand the parts by seeing the connections of the whole.

How we manage a city is in part determined by the metaphors we employ to describe it. If we think of the city as a machine made up of parts and fragments rather than as an organism made up of related, interconnected wholes, we invoke mechanical solutions that may not address the whole issue. And a mechanistic approach similarly impacts on public spirit. If, instead, we focus on the widest implications of a problem, on connections and relationships, we can make policy linkages between, say, housing, transport and work; between culture, the built environment and social affairs; between education, the arts and happiness; or between image, local distinctiveness and fun.

Whose truths?

The new Zeitgeisters value the subjective as well as the objective. If someone says 'I feel good' or 'I feel bad', this is a truth. They listen to emotions and credit these with due seriousness. They look at the effects on deeper psychology and believe these are important in city-making. They'd 'rather be vaguely right than precisely wrong'.[6] They agree with those who believe the notion of a stable, unwavering truth waiting to be discovered has been discredited. Fritz Capra summarizes succinctly the point made earlier:

> My conscious decision about how to observe, say, an electron, will determine the electron's properties to some extent. If I ask it a particle question, it will give me a particle answer; if I ask it a wave question it will give me a wave answer. The electron does not have objective properties independent of my mind. In atomic physics the sharp Cartesian division between mind and matter, between the observer and the observed, can no longer be maintained. We can never speak of nature without speaking about ourselves.[7]

The new Zeitgeisters want to encourage a conceptual shift in what we take seriously and how we view things. Most importantly, they have a value base. It is based on curiosity about 'the other' and so is interested in cross-cultural connections and not inward-looking, tribal behaviour. It believes in bending markets to bigger picture objectives such as greater social equity, care for the environment or aspirational goals. The market on its own has no values; it is only a mechanism. The emerging spirit of the times tries to think holistically.

Being lofty

These lofty aims are not unrealistic simply because they are lofty. Lofty does not mean vague. It can mean trying to see clearly and to give a sense of the direction of travel rather than the name of every station in between. Of course, this scares the pre-committed and closed-minded. Shifts in Zeitgeist are mostly triggered by the coming together of sets of circumstance: an event like Hurricane Katrina or 9/11 or, on a lesser scale, the sudden awareness of a tipping point – the UK government's 'Avoiding Dangerous Climate Change' report of January 2006 makes global warming deniers seem crazily committed to being blind; the Northern Ireland Statistics and Research Agency 2005 report documents coldly the connection between segregation, deprivation, sectarian violence and lack of economic prospects. These 'events' are enhanced by media clamour. Suddenly it seems the time has come for a set of ideas. And the hordes of the new Zeitgeisters are ready to pounce.

Crisp encapsulations

Most importantly, Zeitgeist shifts because it becomes a better representation of reality. It chimes with 'common sense'. A contested term, the idea of common sense has been argued about for centuries. In German it literally means 'healthy human understanding',[8] but can be understood as the 'generally accepted majority view', with examples being 'laws apply to everyone', 'peace is better than war' or 'everyone should have access to health services'. 'Some use the phrase to refer to beliefs or propositions that in their opinion they consider would in most people's experience be prudent and of sound judgment.'[9] Common sense is dynamic, not static, and what makes sense changes with time and circumstance.

Shifting common sense requires the dissemination of the starkly illustrative. New cultural narratives by their nature are more difficult to inculcate into common sense – there are few stark facts or figures that can evince an epiphany. But environmental narratives, on the other hand, constitute a more jarring challenge to received wisdom and it is not difficult to construct out of them would-be iconic soundbites that can seep into common sense. For instance, you do not need to be a scientist to understand that increasing the number of cars in Britain by 800,000 a year cannot continue. This net increase is equivalent to an extra six-lane motorway full of bumper-to-bumper motor vehicles from London to Edinburgh, a length of 665km, every year.[10] The average European car produces over 4 tonnes of carbon dioxide every year. You do not need much skill to calculate that 800,000 times 4 tonnes equals 3,200,000 tonnes, nor that pumping this compound, invisible though it may be, into the atmosphere must have an effect. We simultaneously acknowledge and deny the link between exhaust fumes and acid rain, lead-poisoning and a variety of bronchial and respiratory illnesses. But we don't need much insight to realize that cars, whether moving or static, clog up cities and give them an overwhelming 'car feel'. Is it therefore not 'common sense' to curtail car use and encourage less-polluting forms of transport?

Would-be iconic facts such as these enable the understanding of things that seem self-evidently true. Or do they? Many want to hide from 'reality'. They are wilfully ignorant, their fear often masked behind arrogant overconfidence and power play. The will leading to ignorance and apathy arises especially among the beneficiaries of the status quo, whether financially, through peer groups or even emotionally. It takes commitment to change. The structures and incentives around us do not help, nor does the mantra of 'free choice', two deeply contested words that are used together as if they could never be queried. It takes behavioural change, but denial translates into avoidance activity. With glazed open eyes we sleep-walk into crisis. It hurts to digest the implications of facing things as they are, and to do something about them. The Zeitgeist changes when the unfolding new can be described in crisp encapsulations; this gives the spirit of the times a firm, persistent push, so it appears as the new common sense.

Capturing the Zeitgeist

In every age there are battles to capture the Zeitgeist, because when on your side it is a powerful ally. The goal is to portray adversaries as if they are acting against history in some sense. So, for instance, hardened reactionaries will accuse emergent trends of being woolly or devoid of reality in an attempt to put them down. Today the battles and dividing lines centre on your views around a series of faultlines, which determine whether you are 'one of us'.

The emergent spirit has an ethical twist and includes a concern for the following:

- **Distinctiveness** – fostering authenticity of places to strengthen their identity and ultimately their competitiveness.
- **A learning community** – encouraging participation and listening. The city becomes a place of many learners and leaders.
- **Wider accounting** – balancing economic goals with others such as liveability and quality of life.
- **Idealism** – encouraging activism and a values-based approach to running a city. Not shying away from altruism.
- **Holism** – having a whole systems view so sharing a concern for ecology or culture.
- **Diversity** – having an interest in difference and cross-cultural consolidation and rejecting intolerance.
- **Gendered approaches** – having an interest in the other sex's perspectives on running cities.
- **Beyond technology** – technology is not the answer to every problem. It is not a white knight that can address all urban problems, from segregation to gang culture. We also need to encourage behavioural change, while stopping short of engineering society.[11]

CITYNESS IS EVERYWHERE

The world's urban population has just passed 50 per cent. This is an iconic figure. We are inexorably leaving the rural world behind; everything will in future be determined by the urban. Of course, in more developed places in the world, the urban population is already well over 50 per cent – over 74 per cent in Europe and 80 per cent in the Middle East and Australia – but this is a critical moment, the turning point from rural to urban.

'Cityness' is the state most of us find ourselves in. Cityness is everywhere because even when we are nominally far away from cities, the city's maelstrom draws us in. Its tentacles, template and footprint reach out into its wide surrounds, shaping the physical look, the emotional feel, the atmosphere and economics. The

Source: Charles Landry

The city is more than 'roads, rates and rubbish', as the Australians say (or 'pipes, potholes and police', as the Americans say)

perceptual reach and physical impact of London, for example, stretches 70km in all directions, that of New York even further, that of Tokyo well beyond. Their networks of roads, pipes and pylons stretch into the far yonder. And the same is true even for smaller settlements – each has a catchment area or dynamic pull around itself. When these magnetic maelstroms and catchments are added together, nearly nothing is left of what was once called nature. The overarching aura is the city.

Urbanism is the discipline which helps us understand this aura and see the dynamics, resources and potential of the city and cityness in a richer way; urban literacy is the ability and skill to 'read' the city and understand how cities work and is developed by learning about urbanism. Urbanism and urban literacy are linked generic and overarching skills, and a full understanding of urbanism only occurs by looking at the city with different perspectives, insights and multiple eyes. Overlaying it is cultural literacy – the understanding of how cultures work – which ultimately is key.[12]

Night maps show the extent of urban ubiquity most graphically. The entire Japanese nation shines like a beacon. Osaka to

Tokyo is nearly one built mass, a contiguous city of 80 million people stretching 515km. The Pearl River Delta in Southern China went from paddy fields to near complete urbanization in 50 years. Even more extreme, the seaboard of the east coast of China will soon be one strip of urbanization. The east coast of the US is all but completely urbanized from Boston to Washington, which is 710km, and the lights extend inland too. From the east coast inwards are 1000km stretches of light blur. Forty years ago the Spanish coastline seen from the air was punctuated by a few large cities, such as Barcelona, Valencia, Alicante, Almeria and Malaga with some speckled fishing villages in between. Now it is almost completely built up along a 970km stretch. The same is true for Marseille in France to Genoa in Italy (440km). Only Africa is a far dimmer continent, rarely punctuated by bright interruptions.

The inexorable movement of people, who hope cities can fulfil their dreams, expectations or sheer need for survival, feeds cities. But this is not happening uniformly. In Europe populations have stabilized and are about to begin their decline.[13] During industrializing eras concentration is the dominant force, as witnessed in Europe and the US, with populations shifting from smaller towns to large cities. A second pattern now emerging is a parallel counter-urbanization – larger cities are stuttering, with the largest percentage gains seen in smaller cities and rural areas – though the rebirth of the city in the West is curtailing that trend somewhat, bolstered by attempts to make cities safer, more attractive, vital and vibrant, so enticing various subgroups such as empty-nesters or young professionals.

In East Asia and the rest of the developing world, by contrast, the pull to the city continues unabated, fed by hope and need. We are witnessing the largest movement of people in history. Wave upon wave of incomers are arriving. The vast majority are poor, but once semi-settled there are layers of deprivation within this poverty and each layer has differing economic prospects. In spite of abject poverty at the lowest levels in the booming cities in Africa, Asia and Latin America, each stratum can provide services to the group slightly better off. So it partly fulfils its aspirations. This ranges from selling cooked meals to personal services as one moves up the chain. There is exploitative production-line work and transport services, then building and construction, and finally financial activities or leisure provision similar to those meeting demands in the West. This makes slums complex. They have their own class structure and stratifications.

Imagine the impact of Sao Paulo's expansion from 10 million in 1984 to 20 million in 1999 – over 600,000 newcomers per year. Or, perhaps the starkest example, Shenzhen, a 90-minute train ride from Hong Kong, which has grown from a rice-growing village in the late 1970s to a city of over 10 million people today. In some sense the achievement is astonishing.

Imagine the physical infrastructure needed. Imagine the psychological stresses. The figures are telling, but the added zeros barely touch the impact of dense living, exacerbating pollution, grinding poverty, the urban rush, the ugly slipshod-built buildings or the escalating sense of things being out of control. The zeros do not put across the heaving weight of fates fulfilled or destroyed, the sadnesses lived through, injustices endured, helplessness put up with, and occasional delight.

In 1900 only 160 million people, 10 per cent of the world's population, lived in cities. In 1950 it was 730 million people or 34 per cent. Today 3250 million or 50 per cent are urban dwellers – the equivalent of every single person in Europe, the Americas, Africa, Oceania and Western Asia living in cities.[14] These average figures, however, mask gaping differences. Ninety-seven per cent of Belgians, 89 per cent of British and 88 per cent of Germans live in urban areas, against 74 per cent of Europeans as a whole. Every year another 68 million people move to cities, the equivalent of the entire French and Belgian populations combined. Mercifully, if predictions are correct, the world's population will stabilize at 9 billion in 2050. Population has already stabilized in Europe, and the remaining the growth is expected to come from Asia and Africa.

In 1900 the ten biggest cities in the world were in the North. Now that hemisphere has only New York and Los Angeles in the top ten and by 2015 will have none. In 1800 London was the world's largest city, with 1 million people. Today 326 metropolitan areas have more than 1 million people. By 2025 there are expected to be 650. Many of these cities of a million you will have never heard of: Ranchi, Sholapur, San Luis, Potosi or Gaziantep, Nampo and Datong, Tanjungkarang, Davao and Urumqi. Who would have thought that Chungking had nearly 8 million people or Ahmadabad just over 5 million and Wuhan and Harbin just under? The number of megacities, cities of more than 10 million, has climbed from 5 in 1975 to 14 in 1995 and is expected to reach 26 by 2015. Lagos' population in 1980 was 2.8 million and is now 13 million and

Kampala's population has tripled over the same period. We could go on ...

Feeling and perceiving geography

How does the feeling of cityness come about? Figures rarely tell you how a landscape or space feels. Near where I live in Gloucestershire, 25 years ago there was a clear distinction between the natural landscape and human settlements, whether the village Bisley, the town Cheltenham or the city outside the county, Bristol. The county now has a population of 568,000 and 60 per cent of the land is rural; the growth in population from a figure of 515,000 in 1980 was 10 per cent. Yet car numbers rose by 30.2 per cent in the same period. Add to this a dramatic increase in mobility – people are currently moving around six times as much as in 1950, from 8km per day in 1950 to 19.5 in 1980, 48.2 in 2000 and a predicted 96.4km in 2025. By contrast, travel by buses has decreased from 32.8 per cent of all journeys in 1960 to 6.7 per cent in 2000.[15]

At the same time, personal living space has nearly doubled since 1950 and increased from 38m^2 per person in 1991 to 43m^2 in 1996 and 44m^2 in 2001. This reflects the increase in single person households and the decrease in larger families.[16] As more people demand more dwelling space, so existing settlements expand and new ones emerge. Empty space is ever more scarce.

To accommodate the increasing numbers of people over time, open space was infilled and new estates were built. The greater number of cars led to strategic roads being widened, bypasses being added and more roundabouts. The larger supermarkets were moved from town centre cores to peripheries at the nexus points of various settlements, petrol stations were added along routes, ribbon developments were allowed and more signs were put up. Step by step and imperceptibly the atmosphere changed. The area's overall feel is now one of cityness.

Transpose this tiny local instance in Gloucestershire on to the global scale. Visualize the vehicles and the ever-expanding physical infrastructure needed and space used. The British net increase of 800,000 cars per year has already been noted. In the US the annual net increase averages 2.7 million per year. In Europe between 1995 and 2002, 32 million more vehicles hit the road. Wait for China and India fully to emerge – China has 20 per cent of the world's population and only 8.1 per cent of its vehicles, a large proportion of which are vans and lorries. The 5.2 personal cars per 1000 people looks minuscule in contrast with Western Europe, where it is just over 400 per 1000.[17] If China catches up, the figures become absurd – several hundred million more cars would be on the roads.

Look at living space. Similar processes to those occurring in Gloucestershire are taking place throughout Europe, where living space differs from place to place but hovers at around 40m². Contrast this with the North American average of 65m² or more dramatically still China, where prior to 1978 average living space was only 3.6m². By 2001, with the massive expansion of apartments, this had risen to 15.5m², close to the 19m² in Russia.[18] What are the spatial implications of China reaching European levels?

Single person households are rising. In Britain in 2001, 29 per cent of households were solely inhabited by single persons, up from 18 per cent in 1971. Household inhabitants have reduced from 2.91 people per dwelling in 1971 to 2.3 in 2001. In Sweden, the figure is 1.9, the lowest in Europe. If Britain were to match Swedish figures it would require 47 per cent more dwellings by 2050. Consider the physical impact of these increased dwellings. In the rest of the developed world the range falls within the same margins – the US, for instance, has a figure of 2.61 – but for the less developed world it is just over 5. India has 5.4 and Iraq, the highest, 7.7. Once these countries develop, the demand for space and mobility will increase, although population growth will decline as education levels increase. This is the acknowledged pattern, but by the time that has happened what will the world look like?[19]

Flipping perception

The impact of the intensification of land use and movement is dramatic. The distinction between the natural and built environment has eroded. The balance has tipped inexorably. From a feeling of settlements within nature, there are now interconnected, sprawling settlements within which there is parkland. The nature we have is manicured, contained and tamed. It is a variant of a park. The wolves, the bears and the snakes have long gone. Sad it may be, but better to start from an honest premise.

Even widening a road through the countryside from one lane to two so that cars can pass one another has startling effects. In the one-lane landscape the car is careful, contained and cagey. Trees and foliage dominate. But as road space spreads, the visual impact

Source: Charles Landry

Cityness sprawls into every crevice of what was once nature

of asphalt grows disproportionately, making the natural landscape feel less significant. The dual carriageway finally changes the perceptual balance completely, and this is a pattern seen the world over. To talk of urban versus rural makes increasingly less sense. For instance, the Midlands in Britain and much of the south of the country are in truth series of built-up villages, towns and cities connected by roads; the green in between is incidental.

Transport is central to the equation and the need to think it through creatively is urgent. For example, the width of land surface taken up by a double railway line is only 12m, compared with 47m for a three-lane motorway. A typical freight train can move over 1000 tonnes of product, equivalent to 50 heavy goods vehicles. And around 30 per cent of the lorries are running empty at any one time. Moving a tonne of freight by rail produces 80 per cent less carbon dioxide than moving it by road. Light van traffic is projected to grow by 74 per cent by 2025. Articulated lorry traffic is expected to grow by 23 per cent by 2010 and 45 per cent by 2025.[20] Rail freight accounts for 12 per cent of the British surface freight market and removes over 300 million lorry miles from the roads every year. Its external cost to the environment and community (excluding congestion) is eight times less than road freight in terms of carbon dioxide per tonne kilometre.[21]

Alternatives are possible. The Brazilian city of Curitiba has a 150km bike network linked to a bus network. There is one car for every three people (which some might consider underdevelopment) and two-thirds of trips are made by bus. There has been a 30 per cent decline in traffic since 1974, despite a doubling of the population. Freiburg in Germany shows similar figures.[22] Since 1982 local public transport has increased from 11 per cent to 18 per cent of all journeys made, and bicycle use from 15 per cent to 26 per cent, while motor vehicle traffic decreased from 38 per cent to 32 per cent, despite an increase in the issue of motor vehicle licences.[23]

A *view from above*

Cityness is what comes to mind when you stand back and let the essence of cities seep over you. Picture yourself arriving at a big city for the first time from the air. What thoughts and impressions come to mind?

On the whole, modern cities take on a Lego-like regularity when viewed from high altitude. Box-like buildings hug straight lines and curves while the general hardness of brick, cement and tarmac is occasionally punctuated by the dark green of trees or the lighter green of grass. Sometimes the sun is caught in the reflection of a pond or lake and often a river will run a course. Some larger structures – sports stadia, power stations, communications towers – stand out as distinctive and purposeful.

As you decrease height, activity becomes more discernible. Vehicles move up and down tarmac arteries, the main thoroughfares more clogged up than residential streets. Many of the vehicles are moving to and from the airport you are about to land in. Lower still and you can start to make out people, but watching their busying about is akin to watching an ants' nest – fascination, perhaps, but little comprehension of the activity. Nevertheless, you get the impression of *purpose* as they appear from and disappear into vehicles and buildings. If you arrive at night, you will note the not small endeavour of defeating darkness – billions of watts called forth to keep the urban environment physically illuminated. Cities rely overwhelmingly on energy.

An imaginary journey

How you view the city varies according to who you are, where you come from, your culture, your status, your life stage and your interests. Yet some experiences of the city are the same for everyone. The city announces itself a long way off through the senses: sight, sound and smell.

Take yourself on an imaginary early morning journey from out of town in summertime to a big city, the most common journey on Earth. We could be in Europe, the US, Australia, China – anywhere city-bound.

The manifestations of the city become apparent early on, although you are 30km from the urban core. The once agricultural land left and right is speckled with windowless, uniform aluminium industrial sheds which are, on occasion, brightly coloured. Further out they are larger, the asphalted service areas more spread out, with articulated lorries in the forecourt. Closer towards the city the sheds compact in, they have a more cluttered feel. The three-lane highway itself has an urban feel – an expanse of pounded asphalt that stretches endlessly into the horizon. Compactly massed and close-set cars purposively batter the road, prancing fast-forward *en route* to the city. Some have blacked-out windows so the driver can maintain a private world in a moving sea of metal. It is very difficult to stop anywhere. Later in the day the asphalt will give way a little, especially in the heat, but it is still unresponsive and dead in look and in feel.

Instructional signs begin to escalate, telling you to slow down here, speed up there and where to veer off into suburbs before you reach the outer ring road. And in the distance, still 15km away, shimmering against the morning sun that breaks through the clouds, a high-rise building reflects a sharp shaft of sunlight. You get closer, structures pile up.

It is getting denser – the sensation of asphalt, concrete, glass, bricks, noise and smell mounts and spirals. Adverts swell, passing with greater frequency: 'Do this', 'Do that', 'Want me', 'Desire me', 'Buy me'. Your radio is on, with continued interruptions. That makes 52 exhortations to buy since you left home. You protect yourself from information overload by selectively half-closing and half-opening your ears; but you need to know the traffic news. The car windows are closed, the air conditioning on, but the air is stale, so you need a waft of fast-moving air from the outside. Either way, you are driving in a tunnel of pollution and you are beginning to smell the approaching city. The petrol vapour is warm, fetid and globular, perhaps even comforting. It causes a light-headed giddiness. It is the urban smell *par excellence*.

The hard surfaces of the city intensify. You are in a completely built-up area, but the multi-lane highway means you can zip along. The road has just been widened to four lanes at this point. Now you're in a secure funnel guiding you straight into town. You remember that argument with the eco-guy. You think to yourself, 'I am moving fast. What was that nonsense about *induced traffic transportation* that planners dread?' You recall that this is where despite highway capacity being increased when it becomes congested, over time more cars on the road drive longer distances to access the same services, and the new highway becomes just as congested as the old one was.

'Forget all that. Any problem will be solved in the near future by technologies that are currently *just around the corner*, like satellite guidance.'

The urban street patterns are not yet clear; the sight lines are obscured by underpasses and overpasses. They are made from concrete. Inert and lifeless, they throw an unresponsive deadness back at you. Concrete's shapes can on occasion lift – the swoosh and sweep of a concrete curve – but it ages disgracefully. It leaches, stains and cracks, not to mention cancerous concrete that breaks up to reveal rusty steel, or graffiti.

Reinforced concrete[24] is the material of the industrial age and you are seeing more of it now. Endless concrete garden walls, rashly constructed. Cheap housing estates. Cheaper breeze-block accommodation for the even poorer. A grey concrete car park on the horizon greets you with a garish red sign: 'All Day Parking – Only $5.'

But still there is some green. A tree-lined street eases by in the once middle-class outer suburb of single detached houses. It is now a lower middle-class area with rented accommodation divided into units. A few abandoned cars, perhaps, but the place seems perfectly fine from a distance. It might just revitalize and become the new outer urban chic, maybe for those that moved to outer-outer suburbia and found auto-dependency too much.

Over the last 80 years the transformation from walkable to automobile-dependent has been extraordinary. It didn't just happen. A set of policies at all levels of government have favoured cars over all other transport.

You're on a flyover, which explains why this area originally went into a downward spiral. Who wants to live under a motorway? But for you it provides a vista – you can see the urban panorama. Is that IKEA in the far distance? Closer by there is a colonnaded shopping mall within a sea of car-parking and brand names. You can read the signs from a distance. The mighty M sign is one, the famous golden arches – that's four or five within the last 3km. Then there's Wendy's, Burger King, Nando's, KFC, Subway. BP, Texaco. Wal-Mart or Tesco or Carrefour or Mercadona. As signs they are as recognizable as a smile or a wave. The ads are everywhere now: mobile phones ('Stay in touch wherever you are'), finance deals ('With interest rates this low, who can say No?'), banking ('The bank you can trust'), telecommunications ('Global connectivity at a switch of a button'), and property ('Buy into urban living, the art of sophistication').

You should have left ten minutes earlier. The exit lanes are jamming up and the three sets of traffic lights ahead always cause a problem. You're on the outer-inner edge of town. Brick and concrete give way to glass. The street is segmented into big blocks, with huge setbacks, with forecourts embellished by public sculptures in their ubiquitous red and their abstract forms; these are buildings that pronounce themselves, they shine in glass and marble yet feel as if they are warding you off and keeping you at bay. They are buildings that say 'no', and buildings which pretend to say 'yes'. It's down into the car park. There is still lots of space at 8.15am.

For every person living in the US there are eight parking spaces. That's over 1.5 billion.

Sameness and difference

Suburbia and its discontents

Some might say that this imaginary drive is an unfair depiction, only bringing out the worst of city life. We could have started with a more positive metropolitan adventure – one that skirts the more artsy, ethnically diverse side of things – but the drudgery of the daily commute is far more familiar.

We could have driven the other way towards suburbia, the setting cognoscenti love to hate. One might tut tut at its popularity, but only 17 per cent against 83 per cent of Americans expressed a preference for an urban town house within preferred walking distance of stores and mass transit in a national survey.[25] Similar figures also hold for Australia, and the new world economies are catching on.[26] *Get Used to It: Suburbia's Not Going to Go Away*, as one author titles his book.[27] Polls, Kotkin notes, consistently show a large majority of suburbanites are happy with their neighbourhoods in spite of the bad press suburbs get. Sprawl has provided individuals and families with a successful strategy to adapt to urban dysfunction: failing schools, crime, lack of space and the lack of personal green spaces of the inner city a stick; the ample car-parking and convenience shopping of suburbia a carrot. Why worry about the lack of urban hum? Let people have what they want, the argument goes. Forget the social and environmental costs and, anyway, suburbs are becoming more like towns. As Joel Kotkin describes:

> *There are bubbling sprawl cities like Naperville, Illinois and brash new 'suburban villages' popping up in places such as Houston's Fort Bend County or Southern California's Santa Clarita Valley. There are glistening new arts centres and concert halls in Gwinett County, Georgia. Almost everywhere there are new churches, mosques, synagogues and temples springing to life along our vast ex-urban periphery. This humanization of suburbia is critical work and is doing much to define what modern cities will look like throughout advanced countries. These are great projects, worthy of the energies and creative input of our best architects, environmentalists, planners and visionaries – not their contempt and condemnation.[28]*

Forget that sprawl is an inefficient use of land, with large quantities of space taken up by roads and parking and zoning laws mandating large setbacks, buffer zones or minimum lot sizes; that continual expansion of road systems ensures land is cheap, encourages 'leapfrog' development, and leaves undeveloped land or brownfield sites inside the city; that more roads increase traffic congestion, because it induces more driving; that it separates land uses, leaves commercial developments to ease themselves into vacant land usually at one storey; that it uses up almost exclusively greenfield sites, previously in either agricultural use or a natural state. Forget the health consequences of sprawl – a huge cause of premature death.[29]

Others point out how government incentives and regulations have consistently favoured suburbia, opening up land for suburban developments at the expense of the city core, destroying the urban neighbourhoods through which they pass. The urban regeneration boom that started 15 years ago has shifted the focus somewhat and created some turnaround, yet the shrinking tax base in cities has led to a vicious cycle, with public services such as education and policing far inferior to that in the suburbs. The balance of spending is still on multi-lane highways, bypasses and road-widening schemes, taking passengers away from public transit, with vigorous lobbying by automobile and oil companies lending a helping hand. Low density suburbs are in essence inaccessible without a car. Today's suburbs include office buildings, entertainment facilities and schools and can exist independently of central cities. Dissatisfaction with their physical appearance, moreover, has led to the complex maze of regulations and the New Urbanism agenda that shape their current look and feel.[30] Gridded street layouts have been abandoned in favour of sinuous networks of culs-de-sac, and zoning laws have been extended to address lot sizes, permissible uses, parking requirements, buffer zones, façade treatments and billboards. However, while they may be more attractive than before, their primary effect fosters car dependency, increases development costs, and makes it 'illegal to build anything remotely walkable'.[31] Even the French, urbanists *par excellence*, are into it. Head out to the *grand couronne* far outside the capital, skipping over the poorer, heavily immigrant suburbs closer to the centre.

So far we have conflated Europe, Australia and the US into one and have thus made sweeping statements to get across an overall feel. Would there have been a contrast had we separated out the experiences? Yes and no. The sheer corrosive physical impact of quarter-acre block suburban development is more dominating in the US and Australia. Its hold on the psyche cannot be overstated. Some indeed love it very much. Suburbia is a form of urban development which lends itself to a particular form of description distinct from that of cities in general. The word city implies density, height, streets, intricacy, intimacy, intense interaction. Suburbia, on the other hand, is a new settlement form with its own logic and dynamic spread out like a flattened pancake. Europe is moving towards the North American and Australian way, but we have less space to play with. Advocates play with numbers and, depending on the country, argue that only 2–4 per cent of total land space is used up. Others say that already 4 per cent of US land is used up as roads. There is plenty left, yet some people forget to assess the perceptual geography on the ground. The city's linked physical infrastructure of pylons, roads and utility plants casts its net immeasurably further out into the landscape, so shaping the feel of the space as if it were merely supporting the city and suburbia. In terms of perception, roads feel as if they are taking up a third of overall space and, indeed, in cities such as Los Angeles asphalt takes up even more.

The US, Canada and Australia still play with space as if it were in endless supply. Transportation codes demand greater leeway on turning circles, turn-offs, emergency lanes, lay-bys, parking bays and setbacks. These destroyers of streets are ever present. Flipping the parking to the back and the building to the front to create a street alignment is clearly a solution too obvious. The tired, listless arguments along the lines of 'this is what customers want' or 'it will increase turnover in shops' hold little water when you see the (lack of) vibrancy of these streets recreated. Visually there is a vacant endlessness. These wide roads project a boundless expanse of ungiving, unforgiving asphalt. Inert machines lazily flop on to the tarmac in front of sheds of chain shops, and there is an overarching sensation of sluggishness and lack of energy. The dominant hue is grey, interspersed with billboards and shop fascias that jump out at you, grabbing you by the neck. Their garish, brightly coloured signs create a tacky modern beauty and a touch of originality; mostly, though, it is the dulled familiarity of fast-food chains where those that are getting too obese feed as if from a trough. North Main Road in Adelaide, a suburban car-borne shopping strip, is the kind of exception that excites. Shocking, bold ads screech at you with their alluring plastic ugliness, as do frontages: This is the car sales highway, one car salesroom following the next; then it is DIY goods; later bulk furniture.

European cities are more contrite in trying to attract custom. There are equivalent streets, yet they have a tighter feel; you feel space is more at a premium. Many places, of course, are hollowing out as shopping has switched out of town, as happened some time ago in North America. Britain is further ahead here, with mainland Europe catching up significantly.

The past is a prettier place?
But the older fabric with which European cities can work is a true gift. It gives far greater scope to mould cultural resources. You can

work with layers of history and the patina of ages, blending old and new. You can contain the car and make places walkable, and the density makes public transport very efficient. Yet finding novel, vibrant roles and purposes for the more ancient European towns, beyond keeping them pretty for tourists, is hard. Nothing wrong with tourists, but when there are too many the lifeblood of a city can be sucked out. A place can fossilize. Think, almost at random, of Delft, Rothenberg, Vaasa, Cortona, Broadway in the Cotswolds and thousands more from Italy, France, Germany, Britain and the Netherlands. Antiques and souvenir shops are fine as far as it goes, but is that wealth creation? Going up a notch or two, Europe has a plethora of mid- to large-scale cities which seem to define what we mean by urbanity: Nice, Parma, Munich, Lucca, Lyons, Reims, Heidelberg, Graz, Orvieto, Utrecht. North America has few cities of this type as most cities there were constructed to feed the needs of the car. The great Italian or French cities and the cities defined by 19th century urban bourgeois architecture in particular have something handsome about them: a touch grand but not overblown, not overwhelming in height but manageable, with mixed uses – ground floor shops, first floor offices and residential above. The streets are tree-lined, wide enough to take parking and often boulevarded to reduce the visual impact of endless asphalt. The vibrancy generated can stretch across the emotions: self-satisfied when the bourgeois sense of self is too confident; gutsy when the urban grime and grot creeps in as the poor and better off coexist; and purposefully calm when you know business is being conducted behind façades encrusted with the urban sweat of ages.

However, Europe, like everywhere else, has it share of ugliness: cheap buildings in the modernist vein, inappropriate design, grim outer estates, shed culture at the urban edges. The functional build-ings of the industrial age often had a proud presence and solidity in marked contrast to the throwaway, portal-framed sheds that allow for vast covered spaces, with a built-in 15- to 20-year cycle. Can you imagine the artists and hip designers of the 2030s recycling these sheds for inspiration or trendy middle classes converting them into designer apartments? Another thought. We think of Italy as an apex of the urban experience: the walkable, mixed-use city clus-tered around a historical core enlivened nightly by the hubbub of the *passegiata*. Yet if we only consider Italian post-war settlements, forgetting pre-war grandeur, you sense they have lost the art of city-making. True, the grid-patterned streets and boulevards are leavened by ground-floor uses in apartment blocks. There are messily parked cars, ubiquitous cafés and general hanging around – outdoor life to give the city a greater street presence. But beyond the ring roads that hug the centres and probe into the estates, there can be a dull bleakness to match anything else other countries can offer.

Although there is increasing convergence, we can still contrast Eastern and Western Europe 15 years after the fall of the Soviet Union and the Berlin Wall. Ironically, as Western Europeans yearned after lost architectural grandeur, they rediscovered Krakow, Prague, Budapest, St Petersburg, Ljubljana, Lvov, Odessa and Timisoara, where there were few resources to allow modern development to take them apart, and where budget airlines now ply their trade. Their faded, dilapidated elegance, as that of Havana, reminded people of what their home cities could still be. Interestingly it was often the more successful places of the past in the West that suffered most in terms of losing their grandeur. Birmingham, Manchester and Bristol had their hearts transplanted and renewed or torn out, depending on perspective. Those cities struggling in the 1960s and 1970s boom, like Glasgow, were by contrast able to maintain most of their fabric. Thus the example of Eastern Europe represents a mixed blessing. Grandeur is often preserved through lack of economic good fortune. A washed-out charm – peeling delights mixed with grey clad buildings in a Soviet style – can take some beating.

Some of the best buildings of the earlier Stalin period have a grandeur and self-confidence, especially in Moscow, Warsaw or even Kiev. Ex-Yugoslavia had its own socialist modernism that still has much to offer in places like Belgrade or Zagreb. Kenzo Tange's brash, bold Skopje reconstruction plan of 1966, after the 1963 earthquake, particularly stands the test of time. But as money ran out, standards dropped and an obsessive homogeneity began to tighten its grip, leaving a beaten-up feel: the 'joys' of Bucharest, Katowice, Iasi, the outer estates of Sofia, Kishinev or St Petersburg, the Nova Huta steel factory and its estates in Krakow come to mind. With rust seeping through the reinforced concrete, these buildings are nonetheless difficult to destruct. Here are tired metal bus shelters, twisted concrete benches, concrete cancer, weeping cement, bent metal shutters. Now political posters from last year's election add to the visual cacophony. There are more adverts for Coca Cola, West and Marlborough cigarettes, beer, vodka, the swoosh of Nike and mobiles than a Westerner will ever have seen. Sometimes they take up entire sides of six-story buildings. They are placed inappropriately. In Odessa I was bemused by 4×3m flashing, noisy ads covering the windows and sightlines of 19th Century buildings. And for visual clutter, the surrounds of Bucharest airport must be breaking some records. One senses and knows this was not planned, however – a great deal of corruption and backhanders have played their part. And one sees on occasion a calming relic: old hand-painted giant adverts for collectivized firms. The larger cities at least have some buzz to go with the visual pollution, but less-known, smaller cities like Kraljevo, Ucize, Elbasan, Durres, Nickel, Tetovo, Banja Luka, Bitola and Kosice have less to offer.

Then there are moments of surprise, originality and inspiration. Tirana's mayor, Edi Rama, ordered the painting of several hundred old buildings, using the drab and dismal grey buildings as a fresh canvas and creating a riot of brash colour and Mondrian-style designs to beautify the city and change its psychological state. It is more reminiscent of a Pop Art painting than an urban restoration project. For a couple of years, around 4 per cent of the city budget was spent on paint in an attempt change the psychology of citizens. Rama noted that the main challenge was to persuade people that change is possible. The former artist noted, 'Being the mayor of Tirana is the highest form of conceptual art. It's art in a pure state.'

In contrast, in the drive for modernity in most of the East, a pervasive, new hyper-capitalist style has spread. Cheap reflective glass – if you're lucky, in fake gold or luminous green – throws your image back at you. Sometimes you can catch yourself in the mirror against the backdrop of an old building. Pressed and anodized aluminium, plastic sheeting and panelling, fibreglass, crushed aggregates and insulation materials collude to flimsy, mean and miserable effect. Patterns are cruder, colour definitions as yet still too unsubtle. These materials are not flexible and do not weather well. Bits are bolted on to the main structures rather than being designed in, giving buildings an unrefined, mechanical feel. Modular design and new techniques able to produce larger panels, much bigger than bricks, have made buildings lose texture. The ability to extrude sections and shape and bend segments in enticing ways is limited. Able to get greater access to the West's new materials of 25 years ago, the Eastern European city planners aim to get as much fanciness as possible for the minimum cost. Yet the results can be tawdry and cheap. This was (and to an extent remains) no different in the West across the whole developed world. Its scars splatter the horizon. The buildings are technically fine – they do their job functionally – but not aesthetically. In the East costs remain more important than aesthetics, whereas in the West the value-adding impact of design and quality is now more recognized.

Local idiosyncrasies

Would our earlier imaginary drive have been different travelling into a huge Asian or Latin American city? Again, yes and no. With, say, Japan or India there is a completely contrasting experience from that in the US or Europe. The overall sense of noise, bedlam, visual chaos, dilapidation, trading, traffic, smell and many, many more people lends a cab ride around New Delhi, Buenos Aires, Caracas or Manila a different feel to an equivalent journey in Europe or North America. But flagship Asian cities such as Tokyo, Shanghai, Singapore and Hong Kong rise up like the best the West can offer, if not better. Glass and steel challenge concrete's hegemony. Their fast, efficient, frequent public transit systems far outstrip those in the West.

What is different and what is similar as you take an eagle's eye view of cities across the globe? Mending a car in Punta Arenas, Southern Chile, surely serves the same core function as in Kirkenes on the Barents Sea, Maputo in Mozambique, Kanazawa in Japan, Oshkosh, Wisconsin or Cebu in the Philippines. The same should be true for building a house, fixing the roads or putting in electricity, going shopping, having a break, drinking a beer, getting rid of rubbish or saving something for a rainy day. Superficially doing many of these things looks the same and has the same output: shelter, sustenance, getting by and getting around. The differences, however, are in the logistics, organization, process, technique, technology, management and cultural idiosyncrasy which shape the comprehensive flow of urban dynamics. Interactively they shape the look and feel of cities and are in turn shaped by them.

We have to consider cities globally as an interconnected system of settlements. Chains of causes and effects circulate in feedback loops with real daily consequences on the ground. Whatever locational advantages a city might have had in the past, now its physical and cultural resources, its intrinsic gifts and the skills of its people are all part of a global network.

To consider in isolation a piece of the world urban map, say Europe or Africa, is to ignore the interdependencies. Every action in one place can affect a world away. The shape, structure and stage of economic development are determined by threads of history from past colonialisms to current global terms of trade. In the development rush we rarely stand back and assess the balance of gains and losses in places as different as Memphis, Port of Spain, Bamako, Oulu, Norilsk, Frankfurt, Qatar and Chennai. It is as if only one rational approach counted: the unfettered logic of capital and property values inexorably drives the evolution of cities and their shape, segregating rich from poor and casting light or shadow depending on perspective or circumstance. The market economy has no mechanism within itself that ensures ethics or trust; it is the embodiment of self-interest. Using money values to drive progress to create more monetary assets means monetizing all aspects of life, even relationships. On its own it is an impoverished theory of decision-making which excludes considerations of forms of sociability, exchange and bonding, as exemplified in bartering or other voluntary exchanges of favour. It also curtails the imagination in recreating anew forms of free exchange, cooperation and endeavour and circumscribes thinking about alternatives. It puts its monetary stamp on everything; someone has to make money somewhere. Capital's gleam lies in its seeming simplicity. It works, too, in a way, if you forget all the downstream consequences and look at the world through the narrow prism of 'economic man'.

2

The Sensory Landscape of Cities

What do things look like? What colours do you see? How far can you see? What do you smell? What sounds do you hear? What do you feel? What do you touch? The city is an assault on the senses. Cities are sensory, emotional experiences, for good and for bad. But we are not accustomed to articulating things in this way: the smelling, hearing, seeing, touching and even tasting of the city are left to travel literature and brochures. It taxes our vocabulary as we are used to describing the city in an 'objective' lexicon deprived of sensory descriptives. We thus experience the city at a low level of awareness. We do not recognize, let alone describe, its *smellscape*, *soundscape*, visual spectacle, tactile texture or taste sufficiently. Our impoverished articulation is made all the worse because the city can overwhelm our senses – honking, flashing, whirring, whizzing, precipitous, huge, confusing. Too often, urban stimuli induce a closing rather than opening out of our senses. Depleted, drained and defensive, our field of experience is diminished.

We live in an impoverished perceptual mindscape, operating with a shallow register of experience and so guiding our lives through narrow reality tunnels. The primary overwhelming paradox for those who care for cities is this: our capacity to perceive is shrinking at precisely the moment when it needs to increase. And this will cause a crisis of growing proportions as the individual and institutional capacity to cope with and address predicaments and possibilities will decline. Our perceptive capacities are shrinking because we do not sufficiently recognize or practise most of the senses. By diminishing our sensory landscape, we approach the world and its opportunities within a narrow perspective. By being narrow we do not grasp the full range of urban resources or problems at hand, their potential or threat, let alone their subtleties. We do not connect the sensory to the physical and work out how each can support the other.

Our world is shrinking as its interconnections become far more tightly bound, as mass movement and mobility continue unabated, as economies intermesh globally, and as electronics flattens the distance between places. This is happening at speed and simultaneously, rapidly bringing together cultures, people and ideas. To handle this complexity we need deep and discriminating minds that grasp the delicate diversities and understandings required to operate in worlds of difference and distinctiveness.

Constricted, we understand and interpret the city through the technical rather than the sensory, yet it is the sensory from which we build feeling and emotion and through which our personal psychological landscapes are built. These in turn determine how well or badly a place works – even economically, let alone socially or culturally – and how it feels to its inhabitants and to visitors. Technical disciplines like engineering, physical planning, architecture, surveying and property development are important, but they are a smaller part of the urban story than their practitioners would wish to think.

The senses contribute to a rudimentary form of knowledge upon which our worlds are built. The sensory landscapes we focus on are the five senses first classified by Aristotle: hearing, smell, sight, touch and taste. Yet it is now recognized that this list is not exhaustive. For example, perceptions of pain[1] and of balance[2] have been identified as distinct from these five. Depending on classification, somewhere between 9 and 21 human senses have so far been identified, more (up to 53) if you include those recognized by metaphysicians.[3]

Take electroperception. The city is a vast, dense sea of electrical energy fields and waves estimated to be 100 million times stronger than 100 years ago. Urban life systems cannot operate without electricity; an electrical shutdown will bring the city to a halt. The accumulative cocktail of magnetic and electrical fields generated by power transmission lines, pylons and masts, mobile phones, computers, television and radio, lighting, wiring and household appliances can seriously interfere with the subtle natural balances of each cell in our body. These massive currents criss-crossing the urban environment are unseen, unfelt, unheard, without taste or smell, yet they operate upon us, albeit at a subconscious level.[4]

Whatever the semantics, there is clearly a lot more to our sensory landscapes than we acknowledge. And our circumscribed, cramped focus has pervasive implications. It limits perception, thinking, the way we analyse, what we think is important and the ideas we come up with to solve problems or create opportunities. It pares down our mindscape.

A mindscape is the totality of our thinking: the modes, proclivities and gut reactions of thought; the theories we use to interpret and construct reality; how this in turn shapes all the sensory elements and how these are perceived, taken apart and interpreted; how our mind responds to and is moulded by the media and cultural representations; and how it handles, engages with and uses its own historical sediment and traces. This mind sets the preconditions for our perceptual geography.

Just as geography describes the Earth and the impact of human interactions upon it, deriving as it does from the Greek words for 'earth' and 'to write on' or 'describe', so perceptual geography is the process of acquiring, interpreting, selecting, and organizing sensory information about the places we inhabit. The aim is to encourage our minds to be wider in analysing opportunities and problems and in finding richer ways of identifying and implementing solutions.

In order to do this, the first step is to perceive expansively in order to work with the full register of experience. The next step is to interpret broadly to appreciate the range of possibilities. Intelligence is the capacity to make these two steps, encompassing as it does vital intellectual abilities: comprehension and understanding, profiting from experience, reasoning, planning, problem-solving, abstract thought, linguistic flexibility and learning. As a corollary, there is an implicit need to rethink our narrow definitions of intelligence as merely a numeric, verbal and logical capacity.

It is appropriate to point to Howard Gardner's *Theory of Multiple Intelligences* here.[5] Gardner proposes that people have several kinds of 'intelligence' and suggests that, in teaching, we have for too long given greater credibility to the thinking intelligences concerned with words and writing or with numbers, logic and abstractions. Sensory intelligences, on the other hand, have been given secondary status. Sensory intelligences here include the *visual-spatial*, concerned with vision and spatial judgement, the *body-kinaesthetic*, concerned with muscular coordination and doing, and the *auditory-musical*, concerned with hearing and listening. Although we admire painters, singers and dancers, their insights are rarely incorporated into how the economic or social worlds might operate. Further, two intelligence types concern communication: the *interpersonal*, the capacity to interact and exchange ideas and information with others, and the *intrapersonal*, the communication a person has with themselves, the ability to reflect. Finally, there is *naturalist* intelligence, the ability to understand the various functions of and mechanisms behind life, an intelligence often lacking for those who live in cities and who are often completely divorced from nature. But, given the fragility of our ecosystems and finiteness of our resources, understanding the relation between, say, a hamburger and a cow is ever more important.

The sense-making process applies forms of intelligence to perceptions and a 'post-sensory cognitive awareness' process begins. This is the mind operating aware of perceptions, thought and objects and it includes all aspects of perceiving, thinking, feeling and remembering. This interpretative process is culture in the making as it involves beliefs, desires, intentions, past knowledge, experience and valuing what is significant.

The sensory realm of cities generates strong feelings, and emotions spawned by urban life are not neutral or value free. They are subjective, yet similar emotions are often shared, especially between individuals within a cohesive group. Conversely, while the fact that we have emotions is universal, our culture determines how our emotions unfold and how we interpret their significance, as do expectations, norms and the conditioned behaviour of the group. They affect the mechanics of body function as well as behaviour. Emotions are the domain where body mechanisms and thought mesh, where the physical 'self', instinctive drives and our perceptions, values and opinions collide. This can cause tension and affects how we behave towards others.

It is clear that the urban experience should very much be understood as a psychological experience. And, as discussed earlier, the physical and social environment deeply affects the health and well-being of individuals and communities. Beauty and ugliness impact on our behaviour and mental state; building configurations can engender feelings of safety or fear. People have thresholds of tolerance as to what they can psychologically bear in terms of stimuli.

But we approach the urban sensescape with chronic myopia and thus an ill-equipped toolkit. Paradoxically, this aggravates the problems, dysfunction and malaise it is trying to solve. This feeling of not sensing can dull and foster a feeling of being out of control, taking people almost to breaking point. What will be the effect on the new generation, who have never experienced anything different and are unaware of sensory richness?

This focus on the senses is not about making people feel paranoid, frightened, hyperaware or over self-conscious. Instead it aims to get us to concentrate on two important things. First, how we feel as individuals and city-dwellers in negotiating urban life in order to live well, generate wealth, coexist without harming fellow citizens and collaborate. Second, to care for the environment, without which life as we know it is not possible. The implications of this expanded awareness are far-reaching. It demands, unavoidably in the end, that, as a collective body of people, we change our behaviour and lifestyles. But better to change through our own conscious choice rather than have the change imposed on us through circumstances out of our control.

Seeing the city as a field of senses could be an invigorating experience. Playing with the senses can trigger action; it might generate the pressure for ecological transport more quickly, for planting more greenery or for balancing places for stimulation and reflection in the city. It would force us to ask questions such as: How can the smell, sound, visual, touch and taste landscapes help cities? Bold inroads into sensory fields have already been undertaken by some cities: light[6] and colour[7] have been tackled where issues such as colour planning strategies, future colour, and space or colour and its effects on the mind and well-being are considered. Imagine, if you will, the differences in effects of a city that is essentially white (Casablanca or Tel Aviv), pink (Marrakech), blue (Jodhpur or Oman's new Blue City project), red (Bologna) or yellow (Izamal in Yucatan). Or imagine a city that is black – the darkness would provoke seasonal affective disorder, well-known in Scandinavia where winter light is scarce. Until the 1960s, London was in fact a black city. Emissions of smoke from coal and industry blackened stone and brick, shading buildings with a uniform, light-absorbing black. Decades of scraping off the surface dirt reveal colour and detail hidden for years. The nickname of some cities involves colour: Berlin or Milan are both known as 'the grey city'.

Clearly planners and developers deal with sensory elements, but often with insufficient thought, subtlety or care. Even worse, sensory awareness is strongly manipulated in the world of shopping malls and destination marketing without an ethical aim. The purpose is for people to spend more so 'nice' smells and 'good' sounds direct and guide people. At the very least we should know what is happening – that, for instance, the smell of bread is pumped out in supermarkets, as is the smell of turkey at Christmas.

Sensory resources and awareness are seen as offbeat, without much credibility. There is no acknowledged professional discipline focused on the whole picture and linking these resources to the physical. Planners and architects might argue they take these issues into consideration, but they focus more readily on look, colour and light. Equally, there is a neglect of the senses in education. You rarely discover a teacher discussing someone's sense of sight, sound, taste or smell. As a consequence, there is no related career advice or training or job route. Within schools, the arts curriculum is the main area where appreciation of the senses is specifically highlighted – of those, that is, apart from smell and taste – yet the arts continually remain in the firing line, having to argue that investing in them is worthwhile. The kinds of imagination and thinking the arts' focus on senses and sense-making engenders rarely, if ever, carry into city-making. Increasingly, artists are members of planning teams, but still more as an exception than the rule. Usually, too, they are restricted to the visual, as in public art projects, where all too often they are brought in as decorative embellishment and as an afterthought rather than as part of the initial conceptualization of possibilities. Artists play large roles in urban events, but little as healers of the soundscape or developers of colour strategies.

People within and between cultures perceive and value the senses in different ways. Places will be loved or hated depending on sensory cues. The sensory environment for an older person might be noisy or unsafe while too quiet or safe for someone young. The same differences can apply to people from different class and income backgrounds. A smell is seen as sweet and comforting in one cultural context and as fear-inducing in the next. A smell can be nice if you associate it with someone you like, horrible if exuded from someone you dislike. The sound of nothingness may feel relaxing to a Finn and like a heavy rumble to someone from Taipei. And for each of the landscapes of sense, there are cultural codes of conduct. The Chinese and Italian speak far more freely about smell in comparison to the English. Italians are encouraged to touch merchandise, especially fruit or vegetables, whereas it is discouraged elsewhere. In Northern Europe people tend to touch each other less. Southern Europeans shake hands and hold shoulders more.

Our experiences of stimuli are also mediated by culture. For example, we consider the sounds of animals as neutral and similar across cultures, but this is not reflected in onomatopoeia. English dogs *woof woof* or *bow wow*, German ones *wau wau*. Around the world, dogs *bau bau* in Italy, *ham ham* in Albania, *haw haw* in Arabia and *wang wang* in China.[8] And *woof woof* is definitely not a dog in Japanese. Roosters *cock-a-doodle-do*, *kikeriki* or *chichirichi* depending on where you are.[9] Importantly, though, in spite of differences about interpretation, there are broad agreements on the significance of the senses across time and culture. Drawing back to this essential sensory realm, the aim is to trigger a direct unmediated response to the urban environment (while noting that nothing is *completely* unmediated).

Sensescapes

I use the suffix *-scape* in *soundscape*, *smellscape* and *mindscape* as I would in *landscape*. I want to convey the fluid panorama of perceptions. Building on the ideas of Arjun Appadurai,[10] each *scape* is a perspective depending on the situation of those navigating their way within it and on how they view these *scapes*, how they perceive and act upon them. These are the shifting and fuzzy ways and shapes within which we construct our world and views about it. Appadurai defines further *scapes* which, while they need not detain us here for long, are useful background tools for understanding difficult areas. They include the *ideoscape*, the linking together and valuing of ideas, terms and images, especially the Enlightenment worldview and its master concept, *democracy*, as well as *freedom*, *welfare*, *rights*, *sovereignty* and *representation*, around which political and economic discourses in the West revolve; the *ethnoscape*, the fluid and shifting landscape of tourists, immigrants, exiles and other moving groups and persons; the *technoscape*, the grid of interlocked technologies that connect the world; the *financescape*, 'the very complex fiscal and investment flows' that link cities in a 'global grid of currency speculation and capital transfer'; and *mediascapes*, the representations and media through which cultural images are conveyed. This broader sense of the urban landscape can shape our thinking and precondition our worldview as well as our physical and mental geography. And it forces us to reconsider the maps we need to know where we are.

A map is an image that represents graphically the position of elements in the real world. But many 'real' elements of the world are invisible. We have maps of territory in abundance: some enlarge or shrink space, some show physical features and contours or buildings in three dimensions, some colour-code activities or facilities. Mapping the flows of goods, people, diseases, weather and the like between cities and countries has long been an important part of cartography; any good atlas shows these flows. Mapping information landscapes, the internet, network structures is a recent development.[11] There are a few maps that express financial flows such as those of the World Bank, but getting an easy sense of how the power configurations in the world work is not a straightforward task.

And there is hardly any mapping of the sensory landscape. An exception here is the Noise Mapping England project initiated by the Department for Food and Rural Affairs (Defra).[12] This aims to calculate noise levels and produces noise maps across England. Governments have traditionally viewed noise as a 'nuisance' rather than an environmental problem. As a result, most regulation has been left up to municipal authorities and bylaws and ordinances vary widely from one place to another or do not even exist in some towns and cities.

The car and the senses

The fact that city-making impacts on our senses is no better illustrated than by reference to the automobile. When a city is built with the car rather than the pedestrian – the *person* – in mind, the car underpins the sensory experience of that city. Too often, the urban background of what we see, smell and hear is car-related: a sound wall is generated by the background hum of engines, punctuated by beeps and horns; the lingering, pervasive smell of petrochemicals permeates the air; the fuel-burning activities of engines and the thermodynamic properties of asphalt affect the temperature; and our sightline is dominated by metal and asphalt. But because of the very ubiquity of these stimuli, we almost forget they are there.

But the presence of the car also affects our experience of the city in very tangible ways. Cars are a very real danger that both pedes-

Source: Charles Landry

How many old industrial buildings are left to be regenerated?

trians and motorists have to be aware of in order to survive. If we're careful, we look sharply left and right at junctions and crossings to check for oncoming traffic. Thus, by necessity in such situations, we are forced to ignore the finer details and nuances of the cityscape. Similarly, we are attuned to an entire lexicography of signs dedicated to communicating conduct in relation to motor vehicles. But the interpretation of greens, reds and ambers at traffic lights and crossings can preclude an even-paced, reflective urban experience.

In the sensory descriptions of the city below, it is therefore not possible to avoid returning to aspects of the car. But the point here is not to sound a rallying call against cars *per se*, but rather to remind ourselves how motorized society inflects our senses, our emotions and our *being*. The car sights, smells and sounds that frequently confront us do not beckon or welcome us, or lead us to open out. Instead we tighten up, close in our ears and noses and squint our eyes as we try to blank out the persistent roary growl of cars or the leaden odour of fumes. We then operate on restricted registers of experience and possibility. The tightening up process encourages withdrawal into inner worlds with a desire to communicate less. This is the opposite of the image of the good city life of human interaction, vibrancy and vitality.

Transporting into a past sensescape[13]

To understand the sensescape of cities today, transport yourself back into a yesterday perhaps 250 years ago somewhere in Europe. Subtract the noises, smells and what you can see, touch and taste one by one: the car, petrol fumes, the hum of electrical appliances, air conditioning, grinding mechanical noises, asphalt, tall buildings, the profusion of glass, plastic materials and concrete.

Mid-18th century, a central street like Oxford Street in London, Nevsky Prospect in St Petersburg or Via Condotti in Rome would be deafening. The clacking and clatter of horses' hooves and carriages were so loud you couldn't hear yourself think. It would be almost impossible to hold a conversation. For a while the stone cobbles in London were changed into wooden cobbles to dampen the sound and quieten things down. The side streets would be immeasurably calmer and, away from the city hub, it would be near silent bar the shout of a voice or a distant bell. You get a sense of the back streets of old when walking through Venice today. You hear footsteps and even dogs walking, which can be eerie. In Europe the sound of bells would be ever-present, telling the time every fifteen minutes to watchless citizens. Bells would also call the people to prayer. The bells of each church were slightly misaligned for identification purposes. There were only short breaks between chimes. In market areas, there would be the sound of talking and shouting as wares were sold and other trades plied. There were fewer shops. Horses, dogs and pigs would add to the cacophony. There was thudding, clanging, banging and clinking as hammer hit metal or wood, making or mending things. Near the rivers on a busy day, the human voice would rise above other sounds. The pathways to the riverfront would be clogged up by horses and there would be lots of shouting as boatmen loaded and unloaded. In contrast to today, the sound of humanity would be more obvious.

The smell could be very strong, powerful, pungent and putrid, at times made up of horse, other animal and human shit, stagnant sewage, rotting garbage, interlaced on occasion by the whiff of lavender from a rich passer-by or a stall. A whiff too on occasion of a bakery, but more likely overpowered, especially if a tannery was nearby. Though not every street would have a stench this bad. You would smell people. People generally stank. Hygiene only truly came into its own from the mid-19th century.

There was more wood and masonry around. Things had a more hand-made feel, more rough to touch. The urban shapes were more crenulated and less angular. The hue of colours was more sombre – browns, greys and blacks, even for clothes because of dirt, dust and a lack of washing. Brighter reds, greens, blues and yellows were a rarity as dyeing was very expensive. The height of buildings averaged perhaps five times the human height, with the churches thrusting above as the only high buildings.

The look and smell of poverty would be all over – people dressed in unwashed, stinking rags, scrapping a living from the streets. The sound of disease would have been more prevalent too, with coughs and spluttering joining the yells and clatter.

But once out of the city, very soon the sounds and smells of nature and the overriding sense of the rural would take over. The city was the exception not the rule.

Fast forward to the early 20th century and much of the old smell has abated: sewerage systems are in place, there is a greater awareness of cleanliness and the motorcar has not yet marched its way to dominance. Nevertheless, new smells are on the horizon closer to those of today: smoke from coal whose heavy particles hang in the air and hover over the ground especially on cold days; burning home coal fires creating over time a smoggy filter and muggy atmosphere that would make you cough and choke. Perhaps there would be a background of grease, sweet and sharp to the nose at the same time. Mechanical sounds are increasing: regular grinding, pumping, cutting and banging noises. The city begins to acquire its more angular, upright feel and heights are rising – ten, twenty times human height. Height is especially dominant in the emerging cities of the 'new continent'. Chicago, New York and Philadelphia adopt a template of wide grid-patterning and buildings are built towards the sky, fuelled by an optimistic modernism. The building archetype is the factory, a paean to production. Retrospectively, the factory has a beauty, generates awe and inspires artists to revitalize them and the *chi-chi-ria* to transform them into apartments. Yet in their time, they told a different story. Factories, especially the great mills of Lowell or Halifax, have a monumental quality with their regular patterning, great halls and assembly yards. There is a mechanical feel, people suddenly feel secondary and like automatons.[14] The machinery of city-making, as in construction, becomes ever larger with new types of crane, steel, pylons. Electricity is being embraced with such enthusiasm that

New York builds its first electric chair in 1888. Things are becoming more like today.

These are mere flavours of a past, not a detailed description. They seek to call forth memory, to suggest and evoke. Everyone can paint their own picture. Lest we are tempted to romanticize, they also remind us of some past dreadfulness, much of which has been overcome – disease, hunger and poverty, at least in the more developed world. On the other hand, grim and hideous as these were, they did not threaten the planet and civilization as have today's toxic set of chemical compounds and relentless exploitation of finite resources.

Linguistic shortcomings

We do not have a well-developed language to explore and describe the senses, let alone in relation to the city. This restricts our capacity to experience fully, as only when we have words can we build on primary sensations. Without suitable descriptors, it is difficult to create and work with a rich associational palette around a sensation. Often we have to turn to literature to seek linguistic inspiration. Sights are better articulated because in general we have a rich vocabulary around physical appearance. Sounds too are easier to describe because language (itself a system of sounds as well as visual signs) can be used to approximate them: The *whoosh* of a car going past or the *buzz* of a bee (although, as noted, there are cultural discrepancies here). Smell and taste, however, seem to evade easy encapsulation. (Interestingly, unlike our other four main senses, smell goes directly to the limbic system in the brain. As a result, the immediate impact of smell is unfiltered by language, thought, clutter or translation.[15]) We rely more on metaphor and associations with other senses, dangers and pleasures here, hence terms such as 'comfort food' or 'the smell of death' and the use of adjectives like 'sharp', 'warm' and 'bursting'. Or else, we describe smells and tastes with reference to the source of the stimuli: 'fishy', 'musky', 'salty'.

The language of the senses is not rich enough for describing our cities today, especially when we think of the combined sensory experience together as one. Our language, unless we look to artists, is hollowed out, eviscerated and dry. It is shaped by the technical jargon of the professions, especially those in planning and the built environment: planning framework, qualitative planning goal, spatial development code, development strategy, outcome targets, site option appraisal process, stakeholder consultation, the role of the development board in delivering integrated services, income inadequacy, statutory review policy programme, neighbourhood framework delivery plan, sustainability proofing, benchmarking, underspend, empowerment, triple bottom line, visioning, mainstreaming, worklessness, early wins, step change, liveability, additionality.

The language of what cities look like is thus dominated by the physical but without descriptions of movement, rhythm or people. This visual language comes largely from architecture and urban design. Its principles derive from key texts such as that by Vitruvius, with notions of symmetry or harmony at its core.[16] Descriptions of the visual city come from habits of portraying classic architecture where building components are illustrated: pedestals, columns, capitals, pediments and architraves. The language has broadened somewhat, yet still has a focus on static elements rather than dynamic wholes like space, structure, technology, materials, colour, light, function, efficiency, the expression and presence of a building. Urban design, meanwhile, sees and describes cities more as dynamic totalities: place, connections, movement, mixed uses, blocks, neighbourhoods, zones, densities, centres, peripheries, landscapes, vistas, focal points and realms. But both frequently exclude the atmospherics of cities, the feeling of the look. Does it make you shrink into yourself, make you calmly reflect or fill you with passion? Does it close you in or open you out? Does the physical fabric make you respond with a sense of 'yes' or 'no'? Does it involve you, make you want to participate?

Let's explore senses in turn, starting with sound.

Soundscape

With urbanization comes a proliferation in sounds. Sound can have positive connotations in the context of music, but more is less with the increased roar of noise in the city. It becomes less differentiated and variegated. Put simply, there are more decibels from more sources.

Yet many sounds attract people: the busy hum of a commercial district, the twang of a guitar from a busker, the murmuring of human voices in a tranquil park offset from the hubbub of the city, the shouts of market traders, the hurly-burly of the morning rush hour. If you like a sound, it can trigger pleasurable emotions. If you don't:

> *Adrenaline ... is released into your bloodstream. Your heart beats faster, your muscles tense, and your blood pressure rises. Sudden spasms occur in your stomach and intestines ... thoughts are interrupted and the digestion of food halts.*[17]

Noise created by humans can be harmful to health or welfare: headaches, fatigue, irritability, sleeplessness, lack of concentration and other symptoms where the body screams for help. Not forgetting the most obvious problem – loss of hearing. Noises loud enough to cause hearing loss are almost everywhere in larger cities. Or, as one writer put it, 'New Yorkers (or Londoners, Tokyoites, Shanghai citizens, Romans) are expected to work and live in an aural state of siege.'[18]

Most city-dwellers experience the barrage of noise as a sound-wall which prevents us from hearing distance, space and the more subtle exchanges among humans or animals. Transport vehicles are the worst: large trucks, buses, cars, aircraft, trains and motorcycles all produce excessive noise. As does construction equipment such as jackhammers, bulldozers, drills, grinding machines, dumper trucks, piledrivers and cranes. Air conditioning provides a constant background whirr and computers an electrical hum. So the noise of global transactions is a broadband hum. Shops have foreground and background music. Even in the suburbs we have lost the art of silence; gardening equipment grinds, grates and whirrs. Overwhelming everything is the big petrochemical roar of the car, but we do not notice it anymore. We cannot afford to. We must adapt as a function of self-protection. We are selectively attentive – we try to hear what we want to hear and we filter out noise. This is white noise, the total sum of all noise, the noise we take for granted. If we didn't, we would go mad. Look at people in the noisy city. They knit their brows, they squint their eyes and pucker their lips in a fixed position to shield themselves from and to ward off the sounds of the city.

To make matters worse, the sounds of the city are amplified by the physical structures that hug our street. Concrete, glass and steel create a 'canyon effect' that loudens the growls and honks of traffic, sirens and exhaust from big buildings. The sound artist and urban observer Hildegard Westerkamp sums up parallel developments in modern architecture, as exemplified by the Bauhaus movement, and sound. She points out that the new international architecture that is homogenizing our visual urban environment is also homogenizing our soundscape:

> *Although most likely not anticipated by Bauhaus design-ers, functionalism and efficiency in building design have been developed to great extremes during the twentieth century as banks and corporations have been erecting their tall towers. Artificial control of air and light has become an integral aspect of this type of building design, where no windows can be opened and natural light does not find access. Sonically this translates into electrical hums from artificial lighting and broadband sounds from air conditioning inside, and powerful broadband sounds from the buildings' exhaust systems outside. Modern cities are not only throbbing with amplified and reflected traffic sounds, but also with the 'bad breath', as Schafer calls it, of high-rise buildings... So, the inter-nationalism in urban design has resulted not only in visual but also in aural sameness: same materials, same structures, same sounds.*[19]

The original impetus for sound awareness came from composers and musicians. As professional listeners and makers of sound, they are acutely aware of the sonic environment and its acoustic ecology, the discipline that explores the ecological health and balance of our acoustic environment and all living beings within.[20] It is in large part artists who have been at the forefront of sensory searching.

R. Murray Schafer introduced the concept of soundscape in the mid-1970s and, later, that of *acoustic ecology*.[21] Westerkamp defines soundscape as 'the sum total of all sounds within any defined area, and an intimate reflection of, among others, the social, political, technological, and natural conditions of the area. Change in these conditions means change in the sonic environ-ment'.[22] Schafer noted too that 'to grasp what I understand by acoustic aesthetics, we should consider the world as a vast musical composition which is constantly unfolding before us'.

The goal of acoustic ecology is to raise listening awareness and to preserve acoustically balanced soundscapes. Westerkamp again:

> *Soundscape Studies and Acoustic Design want to strip*
> *the soundscape of its sonic overload, its noise and all*
> *the acoustic 'perfume' that the Muzak Corporation,*
> *for example, has introduced into urban environ-*
> *ments... Wanting to care for the acoustic environment*
> *in the deepest sense creates the desire to listen to it*
> *and vice versa, listening to it creates a desire, or,*
> *perhaps beyond that, it highlights the urgent need to*
> *care for it – just as caring for our children creates*
> *desire to listen to them and vice versa.*[23]

In fact, in Western Europe, muzak has declined in influence, but wander around any shopping mall and you can hear the muffled cacophony of MTV culture and dance music, in place to energize consumerism. Hence there remains, at least in some quarters, the desire to remove background aural clutter so as to enjoy varied, distinct sounds from place to place.

Sound classifications obviously come from music. The main qualities cover *pitch*, the location of a note between high and low; *timbre*, the tone colour or quality of the tone that distinguishes it from other tones on the same pitch or volume; *intensity*, the loudness or magnitude; and *duration*, the length of a tone. Some have enriched the descriptive vocabulary further to portray subtler detail within a sound.[24] Yet it is difficult to articulate the urban soundscape with these categories alone – its noises ranging from hum to hubbub, from din to honking, beeping and the *whoosh* and *swoosh* of cars.

So we have a low *whirr*, *brrrrrm*, *brrrhh*, with changing volume from a rumble to a roar, but always a continuous soft echo of rubber on the road. The more continuous backdrop of motorized sound is interspersed with sporadic interruptions: a staccato screech, whine, beep or honk, the straining sounds of cars going uphill or changing gear, and blaring, thumping car stereos. The occasional unmuffled motorbike exhausts make your ears boil. Sometimes there is a siren or a car alarm, designed to irk and annoy with its high-pitch, unrelentingly piercing whining or wailing. When these sounds cumulate, they crescendo to a roar. There is often an aeroplane above, rumbling with a gravelly roar, and on occasion it rasps with a gruffness as it flies directly overhead.

Cities are always on the move with accompanying construction and demolition: whirring, whining, clanking, drilling, banging, grinding; or the sound of swooshing or noisy crumbling as things fall down. The vibrations even reverberate within your chest if you are near enough.

Extract the car, the plane and construction and listen to the sounds of buildings in isolation, if you ever can – they breathe a steady, long, drawn out *hummmmmm*. The air conditioning and electrical gadgetry give out a coated, dulled *whirr*. If you listen closely, they alert rather than relax your ears.

The sound on the streets is the faint sound of people brushing against each other, a rustle, the patter of feet, the odd intermittent cough or loud exhalation of breath. Some voices break through, though commuters are rarely vocal. Then open the door of a bar, pub or restaurant, and you are hit by a soundwave. Voices can burst out as if the sound had been condensed in a fizzy bottle. A mix of pitches high to low, distinct voices in the foreground, the words nearly clear, sound in the background more like a rhythm of noise. A giggle or a laugh might break through and someone always has that unpleasant, piercing, whiny, nasal voice. Walking the streets at night and there will be a repetitive beat, lots of bass, faster today than yesterday – a basement bar or record shop, again you feel the vibrations. If you want to hear a thousand voices chattering, move out from Europe or North America to the bazaars of the East or the souks of the Middle East.

Really, it is noise not sound that you hear in the city. Sounds are mushed together and it is difficult to pick out individual ones. Rhythm is rare – and a comforting relief when it comes. Moving trains provide some rhythm, the *dadumdadum dadumdadum* as wheels click the joints on the tracks. Usually, though, the noise is random, a hubbub all around. Traffic throws a blanket over the soundscape so you lose the subtle sounds. Rarely is there a clear note. Discrete and continuous sounds simply coalesce. You would have to shut down electricity to hear silence without the *hummmmm* and it is difficult to experience pure sound.

Remind yourself of times gone: what sounds did you hear that you will never hear again with such pristine clarity? Sounds disappear like species: the hooves of horses clopping that you now only encounter in the military parade or TV period dramas; the clink of glass milk bottles on the front doorstep; the clack of typewriters keys on carbon paper; the pop of flashbulbs; the slamming of telephone handsets. You don't hear church bells often and when you do they are not crystal clear, masked as they are by the noise wall. You rarely hear the varying wind sounds in the city. Long gone is the tweet of urban sparrows or starlings, unless you are in Rome, where you might see a hundred thousand starlings in the evening light.[25] Normally you have to concentrate hard and get rid of the noise in your head to pick out a poor miserable bird. While some sounds have gone, others have evolved: think of police and ambulance sirens, car engines and, of course, the styles of music you hear on the streets.

The sound of commerce is the sound of movement: packing, unpacking boxes, plonking crates on top of each other, shouts, self-advertising, the rustling of paper, trolleys, forklift trucks and their high-pitched whining. Markets are a sound and smell cliché, but compelling and ubiquitous. They have a rich sound colour and variations coming more from people than machines, with those from the latter often monotone. While the precise texture of market sounds across continents is different, its general tone is similar.

If you are near a port, sounds seem to emerge from the bowels of the hulls of ships. Add to this the deeply pitched vibrations of heavy containers clanging and juddering on to the ground. The sound is paced and measured in ports; heavy machines don't zip about, although the agile forklifts can dart about like ants. The sense of slow movement is inflected by our knowledge of port activities. The noise of industry has largely left cities whose economies are now based more on service industries and at whose edges the noise is trapped in large industrial sheds. This is especially true of cities in the Far East. But in the former Soviet Union you can encounter industry in its classic industrial revolution incarnation. Often it is silent as the massive centralized plants have gone bankrupt, with rusting debris lying forlorn, the wind on occasion whipping through the landscape causing irregular clangs. I remember a section of the shipyards in Gdansk, the rusting hulks in the port of Murmansk, the steel works in Elbasan, Albania. Then there are the still active plants like Nova Huta near Krakow or the Mittal steelworks in Iasi, Romania. The noise rings, booms and echoes as it hits the metal structures of the factory.

Nearing the city core there is the silent commerce behind the humming buildings' façades. You'll be lucky to see white-collar workers in the cheaper buildings, whose reflective glass returns your image. Yet transparency is all the rage now and behind see-through glass they go about their silent business. They, in turn, will be hearing sounds coming off the streets, muffled and less distinct though they are because of the double glazing. Inside their offices is the sound of static and hum coming from computers mixed in with voices. If the phone is used a lot, the workers hear the private sounds of other voices. More frequently than not, they will be on hold as they wait to be connected. How many times have they heard Vivaldi's *Four Seasons*, which has taken over from Albinoni's *Adagio* as the new muzak for calls on hold?

The sound of shops is chart music pumped out mainly by fashion and record stores. Usually more discreet in the West, there is a kind of social noise contract for which regulations are notoriously flexible. Thresholds of acceptable noise differ from country to country. The loudest street sounds I have ever heard were in Taipei's Hsimenting, a district popular with the young. Full of teeny-bopper boutiques, six-storey high-rises cram in up to 50 shops. They sell every kind of the latest that is bizarre, self-made and imported. On the ground floor the music thumps out from each of the competing stores, colliding with each other. The sounds vibrate underneath your feet as if you were balancing on a lilo and at head level your ears are assaulted. No wonder the sound of silence was too loud for the Taiwanese woman I met in Inari in northern Finland. She could hear her blood pumping and this frightened her. Calmer variations on the Taipei theme can be found in Tokyo's Harajuku, Electric City in Akihabara or Hong Kong's Nathan Road. But the new Eastern Europe is competing on the noise front. Think of Deybasovskaya in Odessa, Durrësi Street and Boulevard 'Zogu I' in Tirana or even Arbat in Moscow, with sounds coming mostly from cafés. Evidently, being modern is being noisy.

The dominant department store and supermarket noises are more curtailed, in the first a discreet hush, in the later the pings of items being scanned at the checkout or the squeak of a trolley.

Places to escape from noise increasingly play significant roles: museums, galleries, libraries and places of religious worship are sanctuaries of quiet. Their silence wafts over the brow, easing tension along the way. Uninvited noises take energy away; silence can revivify and recharge. With time, relaxation sets in. Often people use these spaces as mental cleansing rooms.

Every city has its own sound atmospherics, even if too many are alike. Yet the sound of elsewhere can be enticing, even though it is largely the same. The combination with other impressions makes us hear sounds unlike those we have heard before. Also, if you listen intently, the sound palette of the roars is subtly dissimilar. The honk in one place says 'look, I am here', in another 'get out of the way'. In one, the honk is a quick beep, in another it is more drawn out.

It is rare for the sound of the city to come up at you at once, encapsulating all the fragments, but from vantage points around the world you can appreciate different sound panoramas: the din looking out from Zócalo Square in Mexico City, the children, birds and hooting from the panoramic view of Jodhpur's blue city from Mehrangarhin, or the more discreet noises from the castle in Salzburg. East Berlin once had a special high-pitched, two-stroke engine noise from the Trabants. In Los Angeles the horns and sirens pierce more sharply because the motors there are now quieter. In Italian cities there was far more hooting and beeping from *motorinos* and *Apes*, the tiny three-wheeled vans, until the government raised noise as an issue. One of my most memorable sound experiences was in Sarajevo, where three global religions meet at a point. The main mosque and orthodox and catholic churches are a few hundred metres from each other. Within a few minutes of each other, there was the tinny call to prayers through a megaphone from the muezzin, bells ringing first to a catholic service and shortly afterwards to an orthodox one – all competing for attention. Only a few years before, practitioners of these religions had been slaughtering one another.

When we think about space, not just in terms of the physical structures that delimit it, but also as occupied by sounds and noise which are wittingly and unwittingly propagated, we begin to realize we are far more enclosed than we care to acknowledge. Hildegard Westerkamp describes Brasilia's soundscape:

> As much as the Monumental Axis and the Residential Highway Axis may connect people between sectors or between home and work, acoustically speaking they form two enormous soundwalls that divide the city... The acoustic space traffic on these arteries occupies is much more extensive than their geographical dimensions. The traffic noise travels right across the expansive green spaces into hotel rooms, offices, churches, even schools, and many living areas. The eyes can see far but the ear cannot hear beyond the acoustic immediacy of the car motor ... because everything looks wide open one gets the illusion of space. Acoustically, however, one is closed in.[26]

As an exercise, try to imagine your own city in similar, auditory terms. What noises would you rather not have? Which are an unnecessary, unpleasant imposition? What would you like to hear more of? How can sounds – especially those that grate – be better contained? As sounds occupy space beyond the geographical purview of their origins, we need to think of sound *territorially*.

Imagine music that you like: orderly chamber music, stirring Romanticism, catchy pop, exploratory jazz, whatever. Contrast this with the sounds of your city. How far is one from the other? Imagine yourself as a sound engineer. Reconstruct the sounds of the London of 1660, Cairo of 1350 and Baghdad of 1100. What sounds do you need to add to and subtract from today's noise? Imagine reconstructing the sounds of the city in a way that feels good to you. What would you foreground? Would the sounds be, as in nature, more distinguishable and identifiable, even the intrusive aircraft?

But we also have to be cognizant of the cultural contingency of sound. Sounds mean different things and have different weightings across cultures and territories. Our conditioning determines our response to noise, though it is risky to generalize too strongly. Scandinavians, it is said, prefer less cluttered, quieter sound environments; the Chinese need some noise to ward off the chasing ghosts of the dead; and Americans have become too used to fractured soundscapes typified by the constant advertising interruptions in their media. People hear, listen to, make and want sounds differently. A church bell might evoke a warm feeling even if you are not religious, but it might irk a Muslim. The sound of a police siren may provoke comfort, fear, anxiety or even excitement, depending on context. As travel and migration increase, there is greater awareness of soundscapes, but we accept too passively what we have at home.

As cultures interpret sounds differently, so they also make sounds differently. North American cites have less vocal sound unless in a shopping mall; Indian urban sounds reflect a greater human intricacy – they are more expressive; and Japanese cities have a more focused, hectic feel. Or is that too simple? Everywhere a low motorized rumble threatens. How many decibels are OK? It depends; the sound of a baby crying has more decibels in it than a pneumatic drill. But the baby induces the emotion to help; the drill you want to destroy. Westerkamp describes bemusement at Delhi's car horns. But she realizes there is an intricate system behind the seemingly chaotic noise:

*I realize quickly that car-horns 'speak' differently here.
They talk. 'hallo', 'watch out, I am beside you', 'leave
me some space', 'I want to move over to your side',
'don't bump into me', 'hallo', 'I want to pass'. What
seemed like chaos initially starts to feel like an organic
flow, like water. There is an undercurrent of rules.*[27]

Sounds engender emotions, they have meaning, and they reflect the
cultures from within which they stem.

We could change the soundscape dramatically; it is in our
capacity. Electric cars are already pretty silent. We could challenge
our innovators to invent the silent computer or air conditioner. We
could ask what would a public space sound like.

Did you ask for your soundscape? Is auditory trespassing part
of the landscape of planning? Clearly not. Acoustic sensitivity is
not designed in. It is hardly part of urban planning and development. It is an unplanned sideshow. Unsurprisingly, noise is now on
many other agendas, such as those of the 'right to silence' and
'sound rights' campaigners: The Right to Quiet Society for
Soundscape Awareness and Protection.[28] The World Federation of
Acoustic Ecology, inspired by Murray Schafer, is based in
Vancouver, which perhaps makes British Columbia and Vancouver
the urban sound awareness capital of the world.

Awareness of noise pollution is rising fast. In New York,
London, Delhi and Chennai to name but a few. New York's Mayor,
Michael Bloomberg, put forward legislation in 2005 which will
provide the first comprehensive overhaul of the New York City
Noise Code in over 30 years.[29]

In New York, noise is the number one complaint to the city's
citizen hotlines, currently averaging nearly 1000 calls a day. The
city is developing a new noise code, focused on construction, music
and other nuisance but not the general din of traffic. This will
augment the successful anti-noise initiative, Operation Silent Night.
Silent Night targeted 24 high-noise neighbourhoods throughout the
city with intensive enforcement measures. From its inception in late
2002 to early 2005, using sound meters, towing of vehicles, seizure
of audio equipment, summonses, fines and arrests, the initiative
issued 3706 noise summonses, 80,056 parking violations, 40,779
moving violations and 33,996 criminal court summonses. The City
Police Department is now identifying new neighbourhoods to be
targeted for noise control.[30]

Smellscape

That smell is extremely evocative is evidenced by neuroscience. The olfactory system has close anatomical affinity with the limbic system and hippocampus, 'areas of the brain that have long been known to be involved in emotion and place memory, respectively.'[31] Olfactory information is therefore easily stored in long-term memory and has strong connections to emotional memory. Smell can remind us sharply of a precise moment a very long way back. Perhaps the smell of an old relative or the whiff of perfume that enveloped you in one of your early kisses. A classic example linking smell with memory occurs in *A la Recherche du Temps Perdu* (*Remembrance of Things Past*) by Marcel Proust. Early on in the first book ('Swann's Way'), the protagonist Charles Swann finds that the smell from a small piece of madeleine cake soaked in tea triggers a raft of memories from his childhood.

But powerful as it is, smell is a sense that we have neglected in cultural terms. And it is the one people are most willing to give up when asked, 'Which sense would you be prepared to lose?'[32] Yet without this sense, our sense of taste would be terribly depleted. If you eat something while holding your nose, it is impossible to distinguish subtle flavours. Smell leads to heady feelings and triggers emotions: at one extreme we can smell arousal and sexual excitement; at the other, fear, as the body releases aromatic substances called pheromones. Smells affect our mood quite easily, relaxing us or dulling our senses. As we can detect atmospheres, our sense of smell gives us a strong grasp of place and location. But, as noted, in contrast to the sound or look of a place, smells are hard to describe. They defy onomatopoeic encapsulation and visual metaphor. We therefore resort to their associational relations.

So the smellscape is transient and difficult to capture in words. As Pier Vroon notes:

> *Our terminology for describing smells is meagre or inadequate due to our neural architecture. The parts of the brain that are closely involved in the use of language have few direct links with the olfactory (smell) system. Because consciousness and the use of language are closely connected, it is understandable why olfactory information plays a part mainly on an unconscious level.*[33]

To make matters worse, although we can measure sound in decibels, colour in frequencies and touch in units of force and pressure, we have no scale against which the intensity of a scent, smell or odour can be measured, so we resort to human inspectors, who are by definition subjective. Perhaps this is a reason for the lack of campaigning organizations to improve our smell environment.

Nevertheless, classifications of smell go back as far as Plato, whose simple dividing line was pleasant and unpleasant. Aristotle and later Linnaeus in the 16th century enlarged these to seven: aromatic, fragrant, alliaceous (garlic), ambrosial (musky), hircinous (goaty), repulsive and nauseous. Two other smells have since been added: ethereal, which is fruity, and empyreumatic, the smell associated with roasted coffee.

Smell exacerbates the differences between urban and rural experiences. Smells in nature have a purpose – to attract or repel. Honeysuckle's smell, intensive yet transitory and fragile, often attracts a double take. Rotting flesh repulses through smell, and for good reason. Evolution doesn't favour those who find the poisonous, the diseased or the dangerous sweet-smelling or tasty. Smell is part of the signal world of nature. The smell of cut grass is a familiar one throughout Western culture. Behavioural studies have shown that this 'green odour' involving *cis*-3-hexenal and other compounds has a healing effect on psychological damage caused by stress. Another familiar smell is that after rain. The wetness and force of rainfall kicks tiny spores – actinomycetes – up into the air where the moisture after rain acts as an aerosol or air freshener. The spores have a distinctive, earthy smell. There are also other scents after it rains as the impact of rain stirs up aromatic material which is carried through the moist air. Most people consider it pleasant and fresh. It has even been bottled.

In the city after rain, the air feels polished and cleaner as the rain has pushed down the dust. Dust is a quintessential ingredient of the urban sensescape. It flattens and makes bland the air. Not so much a source of smell, it muffles the perception of other smells. If it has an odour, it will be a composite of the particular urban matter from which it has arisen.

There are so many subtle smells bumping into each other in the city. Unfortunately, most are unpleasant, unhealthy and bad for us, yet the background smell remains predominantly petrochemical, so it is difficult to discern the detail. If you are exposed to it for long enough, the fumes from cars can give you a foggy, swimmy feel with light-headed giddiness. After a while it feels like a dulling thwack on the head. To an avid urbanite the fumes may be intoxicating at the beginning, but then your head starts to swirl. You can wretch and gag if by mistake you happen take a deep breath in Norilsk in Siberia or Lagos as a 30-year-old diesel-powered bus expels its exhaust into your nostrils at the changing lights. Even with modern buses, the acrid smell and taste can be sickening. When you get close to the running motors of cars and lorries, you can smell the chemical activity before particles become charred and olfactory activity begins to tail off. You can taste petrochemicals, but this does not excite your taste buds, make you feel hungry or build up your appetite. It feels empty and disappoints.

You cannot move an inch without petrochemicals. They are everywhere – in petrol, grease, paint, heated-up engines, white spirit, turps, plastics, trainers, households cleaners, cosmetics and glue. They envelope us like a smog. What is the smell of a new car? It is essentially like sniffing glue. The new car smell emanates from 40 volatile organic compounds – 'primarily alkanes and substituted benzenes along with a few aldehydes and ketones.'[34] You slide into a new car and see plastics, fabric, and upholstery – held together with adhesives and impregnated with sealants whose gases are released into the car as it warms. You smell solvents, adhesives, gasoline, lubricants and vinyl. Perhaps you also smell the 'treated leather' odour of shoe stores. Tanned leather smells slightly rank so tanneries add an artificial 'treated leather' fragrance. Some car makers spray this in their cars.

This is a cross-cultural, homogenizing, globalized smell and it blankets the intimate smells distinctive to a place. It sits low rather than rises like gases do; its synthetic feel is almost like a physical layer. Often heat is involved, and the smell rises in waves and convection currents. There are petrol-fuelled industrial environments where the grease on machines leaves a residue and the sparks on metal create a tighter and more tinny scent. This common fume-filled urban experience can be debilitating, irritating and have a degenerating effect.

For a more varied olfactory experience, head to a market. Markets can be thrilling urban smell experiences when not inundated by endless, odourless variations of T-shirts, jeans and other cheap clothing or the cheap plastic whiff of shoes and trainers. It's the scent of food that hits you right up the nose as if it is pushing your head back. This is most strong in a covered market, where smells and scents are trapped and can circle in a whirlpool with their mixed messages: fish and fowl, meat and offal, fruit and vegetables, beans and pulses, nuts, berries and dried fruits, pastries, bread, flowers, and most of all the wonderful smell-world of herbs and spices. Displayed to entice and to make your mouth water, they play on both your sight and sense of smell. This organic scent-world conflicts at edge points in the markets when we move to synthetic household goods, cleaning materials, polishes, the DIY section, haberdashery, and cane and wicker work.

If you enter a market at the vegetable end, you are hit first by the overriding smells of a complexity of freshness. There are too many subtle aromas around to discern individual ones, save perhaps for bunches of mint, coriander or rosemary. And many vegetables hold back their aromas until cooking. But overall, there is the smell of earth, of green. But the smell of individual vegetables is contributing to the whole, especially when samples have been cut to release scent. The earthy, moist tones of root vegetables – carrots, parsnips, potatoes, beetroot; the ebullient, fuller, subdued pepperiness of the allium family – red and white onions, shallots, scallions, leeks and garlic; and the clean chlorophyll of greens – cabbages, chard, spinach, lettuces.

Over to the fruit. The zesty citrus of lemons, lime, oranges and tangerines, as powerful in their scent as they are in their colour. Ripened summer berries, mangos, guavas, bananas and pineapples give off aromas that hint at what they will taste like. In East Asian markets, you might encounter the durian, with its enigmatic – to some, foul – stench.

To many, spices release the most evocative of scents, and here individual smells become distinguishable: the warm, spicy-savoury tones of ground cumin and coriander; woody powdered ginger; the penetrating, bittersweet burnt-sugar smell of fenugreek; the arresting, sweet aromatics of cloves, cinnamon, nutmeg and green cardamom; and the more complex composites of Indian garam masalas, Jamaican jerk or Moroccan *ras-el-hanout*.

Far more confrontational to the nose are the smells of meat, fowl and fish. In many markets, the produce is still alive, along with the unattractive smell of chicken shit and, by association, fear: the juxtaposition of live and dead flesh will unnerve the squeamish as well as the livestock not long for this world. In the meat section the unavoidable smell of death hangs in the air, leaden, thick, dense, bloody, congealed, concentrated. Offal might contribute a smell of urea or bile. There is an urgency about the smell of flesh and blood in that you might be conscious of the potential transition to the fetid and therefore repulsive.

The incipient decay of fish is arrested in ice. Some oily fish like sardines and mackerel are particularly pungent as the digestive juices in their stomachs begins to digest their own flesh. A tinge of seaweed, ozone, a bit antiseptic and oddly heavy, static air. The smell of even fresh fish is unpleasant to some, but the fish water that runs off the display slabs becomes repulsive to all within a matter of hours, hence the need to continuously wash the area. There is not an individual aroma to any individual fish species bar the fresh shellfish which smell of the sea itself. Overriding everything is the superimposed blanket of coldness.

Contrast the vivid smell sensation of markets with the neutralized, antiseptic scent-world of supermarkets. These cultivate the smell of nothingness, impenetrable, empty, blank. Creating the smell of absence is an art in itself – the blander the better – but there is a constant background tinge of refrigeration: dry, sickly and plastic when you get your nose right into it. You are smelling iced water and air conditioning. The non-smell of food in supermarkets is ironic. It smells not of what you are buying, except for the bakery, where they pump out the flavours of hot crusty bread, or the roast turkey smell at Christmas.

Cheaper supermarkets or grocery shops do not succeed in creating an odourless world. More often there is a stale, sweaty odour that seems to cling to grease that you cannot see. The typical shop smell in the old Eastern Europe was old sugar mixed in with disinfectant and lino, which you can sometimes also encounter in a hospital setting. Yet even hospitals are seeking to control the smell environment through herbs, such as the relaxing lavender, as awareness of the power of aromatherapy becomes more widespread. Aromatherapy is defined as 'the art and science of utilizing naturally extracted aromatic essence from plants to balance, harmonize, and promote the health of the mind, body, and spirit'.[35] Essential oils range from the calming to the stimulating, such as citrus or peppermint oils. Increasingly shops aware of its potency are constructing smell environments, often linked to sound, to seduce people to buy. There is an irony in that we pump the air with unpleasant petrochemical odours, then neutralize their smell in controlled settings and try to put back natural smells.

Interior environments are now essentially controlled. The odour control and creation industry is massive. In the West you wonder about the origin of the smell, whereas in a less economically developed context at least you know where it is coming from. The odours, scents and fragrances have uncalculated effects. For instance, around 70 per cent of asthmatics report that their asthma is triggered by fragrance and skin allergies are known to be common.[36]

Department stores are an example where you might be affected. In colder climates they first hit you with a waft of warm, stale air and in warmer climes, a draught of cold. Yet from Dubai to Tokyo, from London to Buenos Aires, the first impression is of a powerful, heady blast of perfumes and cosmetics. With profit margins high, the ground floors provide an oversaturated smell environment. The perfumery hall is full of sales women who have put on body lotion, piles of foundation, powder, scent and deodorant. The smells are different and are fighting against each other. Every perfume company is fighting the fragrance battle, luring and seducing customers into their smell zones. Chanel, Guerlain, Issy Miyake, Dior, YSL. The list grows yearly as fashion designers, pop stars and the odd football player branch into fragrances. The continuous squirting from tester bottles replenishes this heavy petrochemical cocktail. Modern perfumes are constructed chemical smells with a substantial benzene base. The odour industry can create any scent from chemicals and, just in case we get starry-eyed about fragrances, let's remind ourselves that perfume-makers use the odours of urine, sweat and vaginal wetness in their products, knowing it is a turn-on. Their scents are nearly accurate, yet a good nose will tell the difference between the real and the fake. Synthetic fragrances do not linger and have no staying power. Long gone are the days of real constituents in perfume. Everything is synthetic: remember the real smell of jasmine, rose, lavender, gardenia, lily of the valley, violet, cedar wood, sandalwood, frankincense, myrrh or eucalyptus?

Walking in dining areas of cities, you might hit a row of Indian or Chinese restaurants whose food smells emanate from their air conditioning, either by design or inadvertently. The good Chinese restaurant will exude a blend of ginger, garlic, spring onion and soy sauce. If it is cheaper this mixture will include a fullish greasiness, partly inviting but interspersed with the smell of plastic and disinfectant. The dominant smell of Italian restaurants is often that of pesto, the mix of basil, parmesan, garlic, pine nuts and olive oil, tart but fruity. The Indian restaurant's exhaust might smell of cumin, coriander and turmeric, but pre-made sauces which blur distinctions between individual spices are beginning to dominate.

The fast-food chains have a smell of their own. McDonald's, KFC, Wendy's, Subway, Burger King. They mush into one. They are almost sweet, crusty, a slight smell of cardboard, dry. Grease and ketchup liberates and heightens the papery cardboard smell from which you eat the chips and chicken nuggets.

Let's move from the crusty smell of fast food to the antiseptic non-smell of electrical goods. Think of non-smelling computers, televisions and radio equipment, where only the rubbery connections exude a tiny whiff. However, changes are on the horizon to control our smell environment comprehensively. The Japanese communications ministry is investing large resources in creating the first 3D virtual reality television by 2020 to change the way we watch TV. It is proposed to have several thousand smells so as to create any mood. If that is frightening, consider that Las Vegas casinos already pump the smell of money on to the gambling floors: dry, sweaty, sweet.

Cities have their own scent landscapes and often it is an association with one small place that determines a smell reputation. We can rarely smell the city all in one so we can say that a city's smell makes us happy, aroused, or down and depressed. It depends on circumstance. There is the smell of production (usually unpleasant) or consumption which is hedonically rich and enticing. There is even a smell of poverty. Our home has a smell, but we don't smell it as much as visitors do. Going home is about presence as well as absence of smell.

But there is the sulphurous, bad eggs smell of Los Angeles which grabs you by the throat as this high pressure area holds everything in. The same is true for tall buildings in narrow valleys, as in Caracas, that act as a canyon and container so that smells do not circulate freely. And this equally applies in Broad Street in beautiful Georgian Bath, one of the region's most polluted streets, from fumes that are trapped as the older buildings bend in. The breweries of Munich throw out a distinct aroma of heavy yeast: piercingly pungent, acrid, it darts into your nose and catches you unawares. The tannery in Canterbury, England is just as bad as that of Fes in Morocco. Left untreated, the hides or skin of animals quickly begin to rot, putrefy and stink, which is why originally tanneries were on rivers at the edge of town. The penetrating smell in Fes is caused by the use of all kinds of animal products (excretions, urine and brains). It makes you look at the leather products in a different way.

Finally us. What do we smell like? The city smell is that of people, and the cross-cultural issue is ever-present, with this as with every other sense. Different countries perceive the same smells and tastes differently. To the Chinese and Japanese, Europeans apparently smell cheesy or like congealing diary products, unsurprising, perhaps, given the lack of diary products in their diets. We smell of what we eat and that is a fact, but in our antiseptic world, talking of the smell of people is seen as politically incorrect. We prefer to mask ourselves in deodorant. Personal body smell is affected by several factors – the types of food consumed, the use of scented products, and even the distribution and abundance of scent-producing glands in the skin may vary from culture to culture.[37] The interplay of these factors may result in a body odour which is specific to a culture, a city or a geographic region. With mass mobility and migration, the variation within a culture or geographic region is very wide. Equally, within cultures, people interpret smells differently. For some, petrol fumes are fine while for others they are sickening. So people and places have their scent DNA related to trades, industry, diet, landscape and level of development. The 'developed' West tries to sanitize smell, masking what is bad behind created odours of 'pleasantness'. 'Less developed' places smell much more as they are.

The look of the city

When we envisage a city, we are quite likely – especially if we haven't been there before – to draw on previous, perhaps iconic, representations of it: postcards, paintings, maps (London's wonderful though abstracted Tube map), TV programme opening titles (*Eastenders* for London, *Friends* for Manhattan) and news images (where else, alas, can you see a city's skyline changed live, as in the 9/11 disaster?). We may also recall personal memories of arrival – landing close to Las Vegas' Strip or driving into Mumbai from the airport – and catching a particular view, of Rio from Cordovado Mountain or London from Parliament Hill. Monuments may or may not be prominent in our picture – the Eiffel Tower perhaps, or the Sydney Opera House. But in all cases, our picture will be just that – a subjective one formed by our experiences and by other narratives. The look is always gleaned from a particular vantage point.

The look of the city depends on where you stand and its layout. A warren of streets is a different experience, from the ground or from on high, than a grid pattern. In one case it can seem like a maze; in the other, like an arrow with a purpose. Each vantage point from which you look tells a different story of the city. Are you high up or low down? Are you seeing the city from a distance or close up? Our eyes determine what we see. If you are young, disabled, old, a woman or a man there is a contrast in focus. For one the buildings loom overwhelmingly or can appear claustrophobic hemming you in, for the other they soar grandly into the sky. Our jobs, too, shape what we see and what we leave out as we see selectively. The strategic planner typically sees the city from the air on large-scale maps, whereas the local planner zooms in to the great detail. The one sees the city as slightly flat, more like a surface, and with computer technology its 3D shapes come across with the tilt. The other needs to walk the streets and nearly touch the surfaces of bollards, pavements and houses. The engineers might look at structures and ask 'do they stand up?'. The crime prevention officer is looking for hidden crannies where the sightlines aren't clear; and the thief wants some confusion in the space.

There is one eye and vantage point that has shaped how we look and talk about cities: that of the architect/interior designer. It is but one view, yet it predominates. A raft of glossy magazines reinforces the message. They are supported by an industry waiting to sell its product. There is a vast architectural publishing industry and so far more has been written about the look of places, but in very restricted terms, than the sounds and the smells of the city, for which there is no market to sell to. Occasionally you sense the architect and their critics reflect in each other's glory.

Too few architectural critics and urban writers write with the ease and insight of James Howard Kunstler,[38] who reflects a view of city life in its full dynamic. Instead, usually the tone is rarefied, its vocabulary dense, arid, precious or even pompous. The pictures are beautiful, yet lifeless and rarely peopled. The architectural object comes across too much as isolated, as if it had landed somewhat disconnectedly in the urban landscape. This is a reason why the profession stands accused of being self-referential. There is much left out; you are often not sure that someone is talking about a city within which people live. The confident tone and self-understanding reinforces the view that it is the architect who is really the city-maker.

Let us take some snapshots of the look of cities. The sense of sheer compacted physicality is what makes the city so distinctive. It is the first impression. No other structure built by humans is so complex and extensive. On occasion, the largest steel works have a similar feel. The bigger the height and size, the more different we feel. The extent of loomingness is partly perceptual. With a wide pavement and boulevarded, broken-up street pattern, the fact I am 120 or 60 or 20 times smaller than the building is of little consequence. The same is true when I can view the building from some distance. There are other compensations too. I sense a certain grandeur, power and energy. Yet when the public realm does not work, when streets are too narrow and the road feels like a motorway, the difference between how big I am and how big the building is matters. Too great a difference feels oppressive, interfering and looming. But a ratio of, say, one to six creates a dramatically different feeling. It is more comforting because it is more human in scale. This is why, apart from the buzz, we like markets.

Angularity is the other predominant feature: straight lines; right angles; sharp edges, some jutting out; squareness; planes; blank walls. From above, this angularity comes across as a chaotic range of heights and right angles. There is hardly a place in nature that looks like this except, perhaps, the famous Devil's Causeway in County Antrim, Northern Ireland – a mass of basalt columns packed tightly together that resembles a mega-city.

The latest trend in architectural fashion helped by new technology and buildings techniques is to break out of the angularity prison. There are a few more swoops and swerves and rounded buildings. In London, for instance, there is the Norman Foster-designed Swiss Re building – the 'gherkin'. In Birmingham is Future Systems' Selfridges store – the 'curvy slug'. Yet the surface feel of the city remains hard, ungiving, unbendable, inflexible. More like a rod than a bendable reed. Nature, by contrast, feels movable, adaptive, changeable.

Materials matter. Buildings speak to you in different ways through their materials. We notice this especially when they are made just from one material, like the largely unpainted wooden town of Koprivshtitsa in Bulgaria, the cement-clad towns of the former Soviet block, the mud buildings of Yemen (as in the astonishing Shibam, called the Manhattan in the desert), the grey lime-stone of the Cotswold towns, the red bricks of industrial Lowell, USA, or the sand-coloured buildings in Fez. Then the material speaks to you in its full glory. Wood ages well; it fades, but does not crumble; it feels animate, a reminder that it was once a tree. Cement, by contrast, has a deadening patina; it absorbs light back into itself, and its deceptive evenness gives a place a musty feel; the dust is in the air. Think, for instance, of the once grand Shkodra in Albania. It was given the cement makeover in the Enver Hoxha era. The red bricks in older towns have blemishes; they felt already weathered when new. Colour variations seep through the bricks and there seems to be a story in each one. New brick buildings are too smooth and mechanical; the up-to-date chemical processes of brick-making have evened out the surface and given them a lifeless, impenetrable shine. And they come in non-brick colours: every hue of yellow, terracotta and red.

We live in the age of glass. Glass and mirror have come into the frame with new techniques of heating and air conditioning. The reflective buildings that mirror themselves back at you in a 'look at me' kind of way seem impertinent and self-imposing. To the Western eye they now look cheap and garish, but to the post-Soviet eye they are like modernity *par excellence*. This has come in phases as new materials emerged and were tried out. The sturdy sickly brown and green glass feel; then the reflective golden touch for the attention seekers; and now the predominant silver that throws back clear mirror images. They do not invite nor have a conversation with you, the passer-by. They assert, aggressively, their presence.

The West favours more the transparent look of see-through glass. At its best it projects a sense of democracy and modernity. It feels airy, open, cool and uplifting. When done well the steel and metal buildings combine strength and lightness. The Pompidou Centre in Paris was one of the first of that generation, followed shortly afterwards by I. M. Pei's Louvre Pyramid. Now the style is commonplace and the Toronto Eaton Centre stands out as an example from a cold climate. At night, of course, glass refracts light differently than a brick building. For how long will glass stay as the material of choice for malls, museums and city halls?

Colour is everywhere. It is all-embracing and in every culture. Meaning is attributed to each colour. There is a difference between the psychological effect of a colour and its symbolism. For instance, green is symbolically associated with envy, while psychologically it denotes balance. One does not need to be a specialist to understand instantly that colour shapes how you feel. Dark colours can depress, and darkness has become a metaphor for negatives like evil, ignorance and mental gloom. Light colours lift; again, word associations reinforce our perceptions – light and enlightenment. If a city were to be black it would be depressing, and the blackened industrial cities of industrial Britain were depressing in their time – and grey is not too uplifting either. It was always said that Berlin and Milan were grey cities, which is why their more recent creative and fashionable associations also change how you think of what their colour might be.

Until very recently the colour and the palette used was limited – you rarely saw a green, purple, bright yellow or blue building. The new coloured glasses are changing that, such as Herzog de Meuron's Laban dance centre in London, clad by sheets of multi-coloured glass. The new Musée du Quai Branly of indigenous art in Paris by Jean Nouvel is another. It is a kaleidoscopic, anarchic montage of structures that will annoy those who love Paris's considered order. It clashes well with the exterior of the administration building, which is swallowed up by a vertical carpet of exotic plants punctured by big windows. The hydroponic green building feels as if it is alive – a sharp contrast to most buildings, which feel inert.

Clearly the local materials determined the colour of a place in the past; today this is far less apparent as materials are moved around with ease, with sheet glass and cement the overriding materials in use. Think of the 'granite city' of Aberdeen in Scotland; it wears its sobriquet with pride, but the grey, silvery stone material is unforgiving. Do its colour, weight and heavy density determine the character of Aberdonians? The predominant hues in Mediterranean countries were variations of terracotta going into sandy beiges. It is pleasing on the eye in that sunny light.

Many Italian cities are an exception in having widespread colour strategies as part of planning. There are the famous coloured cities of the world which show how paint has an impact: the pink city of Marrakech and, nearby, the blue and white town of Essaouira, or the blue city of Jodphur in India. The vivid colours of painted houses of Latin America, equally, both shape and respond to character. The crisp colour combinations on the corrugated iron buildings in the once seedy La Boca in Buenos Aires has become so fashionable that it has become the city's design template. Designer articles, from sheets and pillows to furniture, seem to carry the imagery. Did the impoverished residents of La Boca ever get a royalty? I doubt it.

Overriding everything – and again we cannot avoid the greys and blacks – is the colour of roads on which the buildings sit as if bedded in a sea of asphalt. Grey is the canvas on top of which the city plays itself out. The buildings do not feel independent. Asphalt's homogenizing feel shrouds the city at ground level in a veil interspersed by signage and yellow and red traffic lines.

Advertising hoardings increasingly shape the look of the city as they expand in size and impact. Less discreet than a decade ago, they can be immense – the largest billboard in the world, erected in Manila in 2005, was 50m long and 50m high. Occasionally beautiful and often intrusive, it is Eastern Europe that sets new standards of garishness, impact and boldness, and the Far East has always been visually wild to Western eyes. Think of Tokyo's electric city, Hong Kong's Nathan Road or Delhi's Chandri Chowk – you choke in colour and sign overload.

The city is increasingly a sign system and a message board. It is a staging set communicating products and images to you. But it all depends where you are. The colours and materials used in commercial districts vary. In the upscale parts things are more discreet and materials obviously better. The hues in modern settings, in part because of the mass of glass, have a light blue, light yellow translucent overlay. Think here of the new 101 district in Taipei, where the world's largest skyscraper stands. The more downmarket places screech their colours at you.

A business district communicates differently. There is more black – usually shiny black marble – as this is the colour of authority and power. It comes across, too, as stylish and timeless, because black makes things appear thinner and sleeker (a reason for its popularity in clothing). Increasingly, too, blue is coming in. It is tranquil and in control, but blue can also be cold and calculating. Silver has a sharpish clarity, and again it creates a distance between the viewer and passer-by – it reflects back at you. And glass, glass, glass – it is the gloss of corporate openness. Brown is less in evidence now, unless left over from a former period. It looks murky, unclear, unfocused.

A housing or apartment block area can be as different as the country or city it is in, so it is difficult to generalize across cultures and places even though the homogenizing process continues unabated. Suffice it to say it depends on land costs and availability. The denser city will compact building upwards, as in Hong Kong or Singapore, but where people feel land is limitless – as in Melbourne, for example – the city spreads out into endlessness. In denser places, people spill out into the streets as if pushed out of their buildings. The rising numbers of the middle classes in places such as Russia, Turkey or India are creating new, largely gated, edge-of-town settlements in dinky, post-modern apartments, typically 10–20 stories high. The message here is one of 'lifestyle'.

Buildings will reflect the past, particular regional styles, the materials available at various times in history, power relations, class, their function. Often, a principle of city design will inform and order these buildings into a particular layout that affects our visual experience of the city, such as the grid systems of America. Regarding the grid, this tyranny of the shortest distance can have a uniform beauty. But when combined with architectural monotony, it can be dull and oppressive. Green spaces contribute to a city's quality of life, but remember that a green impression of a city can be misleading – much of London's 'green' is private gardens, for example.

Whatever the colours, materials and layout of a city, the climate remains a check on our visual experience of it. A blanket of snow transforms a city; a shroud of mist (or, worse, smog) can hide its vista; and a serious flood can render the cityscape totally unfamiliar to even its own inhabitants. Cities look different depending on whether it is sunny, gloomy or rainy. And above all, light plays on the physical structures that make a city.

How different does Helsinki look in winter, when bereft of natural light, than in summer, when the days are long? Light changes all, and that includes the man-made. Electricity must be seen as pivotal in the history of urban spaces. Artificial light illuminates the dark and allows activities that were previously confined to the day to continue into the night. Light facilitates the 24-hour city. It can also, unfortunately, dull the pleasure of a starry night sky as we unwittingly illuminate particles in the air above with light pollution. More positively, light can make a street look safer at night and can transform the façades of otherwise dull buildings. It can allow us to watch a football match in the evening. A well-lit or sparkling city view can be inspiring.

Lighting has been discovered as a resource to enliven the city.

Some cities (such as Naples) have recognized the power of light and have specific light strategies. Against the chaotic background of the changing city, every new public lighting scheme illuminates a complex clash of priorities and agendas. How can public lighting create an image for the city as well as support urban renewal? How can safety and security needs be reconciled with a desire for visual communication and delight?

A new way of looking at urban lighting, based on a relationship between identification and regeneration on any given site, can be expressed through three stages: light marketing, light art and light landscape. Centrepoint and its environs in central London were adopted as a 'laboratory' from which to evolve and test out a set of generic strategies and tactics. The research demonstrates the ability of lighting to transform our urban spaces at different levels – and to generate and communicate powerful new spatial identities within our nocturnal environments that underpin the urban regeneration process.

The visual environment should be public property, but there are vast differences in how it's thought through. Illumination, of course, is central to advertising and its flashing, bright visual interjections are forced upon us. Japan, notoriously, has a lightscape dominated by brand and advertising messages. This isn't necessarily a bad thing in itself, but we must be careful in matters of deregulation that our cities do not lose overall control over their lighting.

These pages have provided a short treatment of the city's look. There is much more to explore. For instance, we have concentrated on the *outdoor* look of places when there is much to say about the *indoor* life of cities, especially in cold climates. We could have explored the *underground* world of some cities, their metros and subways. Nevertheless, the salient point of this entire section on the senses is that the city is a sensory experience and this should never be overlooked when thinking about a city's future. Above all else, we see, hear, smell, touch and taste the city.

3

Unhinged and Unbalanced

THE CITY AS A GUZZLING BEAST

Stark images like those in *One Planet Many People: Atlas of our Changing Environment* by the UN Environment Programme can sear into your mind.[1] Everywhere you look there is *cityness*. It has invaded our landscape, so shaping our mindscape. Comprised of time-series satellite images of the globe over the last few decades, the images provide powerful visual testimony to our increasing dominion over the planet. Considered ecologically, these images should sound alarm bells: industrialization and agriculture sweeping over indigenous flora and fauna, water resources shrinking, deserts increasing. Most strikingly, they show the irresistible growth of urban areas.

While half of us now live in cities, this will reach two-thirds of a 9 billion world population by 2050. While the city can signify a triumph over nature, urban dwellers exact more of the Earth's resources than their rural counterparts. In fact, there is not enough planet to support the Western lifestyle.

We will show below the implications for resources of running a London lifestyle, which requires three Earths to meet its demands. The Los Angeles population, meanwhile, with their meat-heavy diets and car-embracing culture is, per capita, even more voracious. Six billion people living like Los Angelinos would require five planets. Living like Dubai perhaps ten.[2] Even many rural existences need more than one planet, and indigenous lifestyles are in the minority in terms of being sustainable.

The city is a massive logistical endeavour. It as an overwhelming input/output machine, a voracious beast guzzling in, defecating out. It stands at the apex of the global nexus of goods distribution. Like any living organism, the city consumes food and water, expends energy and produces waste. Cities require bricks, mortar, cement, lime, steel, glass and plastics to generate and renew their physical presence. Then manufactured goods – fridges, clothes, televisions, washer-driers, books, CDs, cars – are used, exhausted and eventually expelled as carbon dioxide, ash or simply junk to be buried out of view. Increasingly, too, goods travel greater distances between their places of origin and consumption end points, using a complex global distribution system of massive supertankers, lorries, airplanes, trains, containers, warehouses, cranes, forklift trucks, pipes and wires, not to mention a workforce coordinated by increasingly sophisticated and powerful logistics companies.

In the following sections I have used quantitative measures to get the feel of the urban endeavour across viscerally. Throwing these figures at you might give you a headache, but please bear with me. They reveal the folly of our lifestyles, the irrationality of our production systems and built-in inefficiencies, notwithstanding ecological impact. They starkly raise the question, 'Can civilization continue in this way?' And the answer is, 'No.'

Everything we do is implicated in the consumption of resources reliant on supply chains. Consider a morning routine: (1) having a cup of tea; (2) morning ablutions; (3) having breakfast; (4) putting out the rubbish; and (5) taking the metro to work.

The logistics of a cup of tea

We start the day with a cup of tea, and Londoners drink enough tea or coffee to fill eight Olympic-size swimming pools every day. The UK drinks 165 million cups per day, or 62 billion cups per year, which is 23,000 Olympic-size swimming pools. You put the kettle on. A standard kilowatt kettle uses some 80 (food) calories to come to the boil, about the same as the potential energy stored in five teaspoons of sugar. In a year, London consumes some 132,769,103,200,000 calories or 154,400 gigawatt-hours of electricity, the equivalent of 13,276,000 tonnes of oil. This is more than Ireland consumes and about the same as Portugal or Greece.

Half the tea consumed in London comes from East Africa, the rest mostly from the Indian subcontinent, China or Indonesia. It gets to Britain packed in either foil-lined paper sacks or tea chests, in containers, by ship, in three to five weeks. In Britain, it is delivered to blending and packaging centres, and packets of loose leaves or tea bags are distributed to retail shelves. Ninety-five per cent of tea is consumed in tea bags. Most likely, milk will be added – 25 per cent of the milk consumed in Britain is taken with tea; 674,000 tonnes of milk and cream are consumed in a London year, or approximately 240 Olympic swimming pools.[3]

In the UK there are 2,251,000 dairy cows producing 14,071,000,000 litres of milk a year. This easily makes the UK self-sufficient in milk. However, because of the idiosyncrasies of international trade, countries import and export the same product at the same time. In 1997, the UK imported 126 million litres of milk and exported 270 million litres. Imports are now less, and exports greater, but 2002 still saw more than 70 million litres come into the country.[4]

Washing and toilet flushing

Shortage of water is emerging as a global crisis and many predict that the wars of the future will be fought over control over water. Water gets to us through a daunting network of pipes to households and Londoners use approximately 155 litres a day each, compared to the average for England of 149 litres, a third of which is used flushing the toilet. An American uses more than treble the amount, while the average African uses only 50 litres a day.[5] In taking a 5-minute shower, we use about 35 litres of water, over twice this amount if we have a bath. Brushing our teeth while leaving the tap on uses 6 litres, a washing machine cycle 100 litres, while a tap left dripping for a day sees 4.1 litres of water go down the plughole. And water waste happens at the infrastructural as well as the individual level. In 2000 water consumption in London reached 866 billion litres, of which 50 per cent was delivered to households. The volume of water lost through leakages (239 billion litres or 28 per cent) was more than the total amount of water used by the commercial and industrial sectors (195 billion). In Manila some 58 per cent of water is lost to leaks or illegal tappings. In Istanbul vendor water is 10 times as expensive as the public rate; in Bombay it is 20 times as much. In developed countries an average of 15,000 litres of treated, safe drinking water is used to flush 35kg of faeces and 500 litres of urine per person per year.[6]

Food and eating

On an average day Londoners might eat over 3 million eggs in one form or another and the equivalent of about 350,000 large (800g) loaves of bread. As a nation, Britons eat nearly 10 billion eggs a year – 26 million every day – which placed end to end would reach from the Earth to the moon. Londoners consume 6,900,000 tonnes of food per annum. A good portion goes through Smithfield, which sells 85,000 tonnes of meat a year, and Billingsgate, which sells 35,000 tonnes of fish. Between 700 and 750 million broiler chickens (chickens bred for their meat) are reared and slaughtered each year in the UK. When eating out, Londoners consume 74 per cent more ethnic food, 41 per cent more fish and 137 per cent more fruit than the British average.[7]

Vast amounts of water are consumed by agriculturists and horticulturalists to keep their crops alive, healthy and growing, not to mention fertilizers and pesticides. Animal farming impacts even more. For cattle raised in feedlots, it takes roughly 7 pounds of grain to add a pound of live weight to the animal. Seventy per cent of the grain produced in the US and 40 per cent of the world's supply is fed to livestock, largely to satisfy burger demand in fast-food chains.[8] To produce 1 pound of beef, a cow has produced 0.5 pounds of methane, a very potent greenhouse gas, which is equivalent to 10.5 pounds of CO_2. The beef eaten by the average American in a year has produced the methane equivalent of 1.4 tonnes of carbon dioxide.[9]

To get on to supermarket and shop shelves, food travels ever greater distances to sate multicultural and metropolitan tastes. Of the 7 million tonnes of food consumed by Londoners each year, 80 per cent is imported from outside the UK. Over half of the vegetables and 95 per cent of the fruit Londoners eat is imported.[10] Each tonne of food in London has travelled approximately 640km. Therefore, 3,558,650,000,000 tonne-km of road freight was required to meet London's food demands.[11] Even though the UK is able to grow lettuces throughout the year, imports increased from 21.8 per cent of the total supply in 1987 to 47.1 per cent in 1998. Nearly a quarter of all lettuces imported into the UK come from Spain. For every calorie of carrot flown from South Africa, we use 66 calories of fuel. For every calorie of iceberg lettuce flown in from Los Angeles we use 127 calories of fuel.[12] The food chain, including agriculture, processing and transport, contributes at least

---

THE LONG-DISTANCE LUNCH

A traditional Sunday lunch could easily have travelled 25,000 miles if a chicken from Thailand and fresh vegetables from Africa are included in a supermarket shopping basket. The trend for supermarkets to source food from overseas that could well be grown in the UK is the problem. In Britain the distance food is transported increased 50 per cent between 1978 and 1999.

- Chicken from Thailand: 10,691 miles by ship
- Runner beans from Zambia: 4912 miles by plane
- Carrots from Spain: 1000 miles by lorry
- Mangetouts from Zimbabwe: 5130 miles by plane
- Potatoes from Italy: 1521 miles by lorry
- Sprouts from Britain: 125 miles by lorry
- Transport of imported goods from port of entry to distribution centre: 625 miles
- Transport from distribution centres to supermarket: 360 miles
- **Total: 26,234 miles**

However, choosing seasonal products and purchasing them locally at a farmers' market, for instance, could reduce the total distance to 376 miles, 1/66th of the distance of the meal above.[13]

---

22 per cent of the UK's greenhouse gas emissions, according to one estimate.[14] Conversely, many high-density cities in the developing world produce up to 30 per cent of food production within their city boundaries.

Rubbish

Around one third of food grown for human consumption in the UK ends up in the rubbish bin and Britain throws away £20 billion worth of unused food every year, equal to five times its spending on international aid and enough to lift 150 million people out of starvation.[15] Seventeen million tonnes of food is ploughed into Britain's landfill sites every year.[16]

Meanwhile, food is increasingly packaged using plastics, metal and paper products. A typical London household generates around 3–4kg of packaging waste per week. It is estimated that London households produce approximately 663,000 tonnes of packaging waste per annum, of which 67 per cent is food packaging. A quarter of the overall waste we produce is packaging.[17] For every tonne of food consumed in York, a quarter of a tonne of packaging is produced.[18] Londoners consume approximately 94 million litres of mineral water per annum. Assuming all bottles were 2-litre, this would give rise to 2260 tonnes of plastic waste. A bottle of Evian, the top-selling brand, travels approximately 760km from the French Alps to the UK.[19]

In total, the average Londoner throws away more than seven times their own weight in rubbish every year and a London household produces a tonne of rubbish in that time, the weight of a family car. Londoners produce enough waste to fill an Olympic swimming pool every hour or to fill the Canary Wharf tower every ten days. London's waste is transported to 17 main municipal solid waste transfer stations, 45 civic amenity sites, 2 incinerators, 23 recycling centres, 2 compost centres, 18 landfill sites and 2 energy-from-waste plants. Of the 17 million tonnes produced by the capital, 4.4 million is collected by councils. Seventy per cent of this waste travels more than 120 kilometres. For every million tonnes of waste generated in London, approximately 100,000 waste vehicle journeys are required.[20] Developed countries produce as much as up to six times the amount of waste of developing countries.

English-speaking cities are almost linguistically predisposed to treat waste as a nuisance rather than a resource, perhaps thus adopting an 'out of sight, out of mind' approach to waste. Seventy-three per cent of London's waste goes to landfill, 19 per cent is incinerated, and 8 per cent recycled or composted. Overall the UK recycles 23 per cent of waste; in the Netherlands the figure is 64 per cent and in Germany 57 per cent.[21] Ninety per cent of all of London's landfill goes to areas outside London.

Perhaps the most recognizable landfill site in the world is Fresh Kills Landfill on Staten Island, New York. The site covers 2200 acres and mounds range in height from 90 to approximately 225 feet. The result of almost 50 years of land filling, primarily of household waste, it is estimated to contain some 100 million tonnes of garbage. Now Fresh Kills is permanently closed, New York's rubbish is sent to landfill sites in New Jersey, Pennsylvania and Virginia, some of them 300 miles away.

Over 333,000 disposable nappies are buried every day in Essex landfill sites alone.[22] Approximately 1.7 million nappies are used every day in London, which equates to around 202 tonnes of waste per day or 74,000 tonnes per annum; 75 per cent (55,000 tonnes) of this is sewage.[23]

The number of live births in London in 2001 was 104,000. This equates to a total weight of 354 tonnes (assuming the average weight of a newborn is 3.4kg). The number of deaths in London in for the same year was 58,600. This equates to a total weight of 4160 tonnes (assuming the average adult weight is 71kg). The dead are buried in 124 municipal cemeteries, 12 Jewish, 3 Roman Catholic, 1 Church of England, 1 Muslim cemetery and 9 operational private cemeteries.[24] London's cemeteries are running out of burial space. Central London, Hackney, Camden and Tower Hamlets will run out of space within five years.

Pollution keeps the death rate up. On the Marylebone Road on 28 July 2005, one of the hottest days of the year, NO_x levels rose to 1912 micrograms per cubic metre, the equivalent of motorists and pedestrians breathing in four cigarettes a minute. Normal daily exposure to London's air is equivalent to smoking 15 cigarettes. In pollution hotspots like the Marylebone Road, daily vehicle emissions are so concentrated that pedestrians and those with offices or homes on the roadside are exposed to the NO_x equivalent of more than 30 cigarettes a day. Other affected areas include King's Road (29 cigarettes a day) and Hammersmith Broadway (27.3 cigarettes).[25] Consider Kolkata, where the pollution in cigarette equivalents is over 40, or the far more polluted Chinese and Russian cities.[26]

Disposal or reuse of waste apart, there is the cosmetic matter of street cleaning. Fast-food lovers, smokers and gum-chewers keep council workers employed cleaning up after them. It is estimated that three-quarters of the British population chew gum regularly. They buy 980 million packs a year, and spit out more than 3.5 billion pieces – most of which they dispose of 'inappropriately'. On any given day, there are as many as 300,000 pieces of gum stuck to Oxford Street.[27]

Transport

About a billion trips are made on the London Underground each year, 70 per cent more than in 1980.[28] Four thousand London Underground carriages whiz around 408km of route (181 in tunnels), travelling at an average speed of 32km per hour, including

Source: Charles Landry

Cars being the priority, pedestrians have to adapt

stops. The metro uses 1091 gigawatt-hours of electric power a year – less than 1 per cent of the total for London.

On the surface things move more slowly: inner London traffic speeds are between 19 and 24km per hour (9–15 km per hour in the worst areas) and 30 per cent of a typical peak-time journey is spent stationary.[29] In the major cities of the European Union the average speed is 15km per hour. This is no better than 200 years ago. Of 11 million daily car journeys in London, just under 10 per cent are of less than one mile. London has the highest concentration of cars in the UK at ten times the average – 1500 cars per km² compared with an average of 150 cars per km² for the regions.[30]

Each weekday, 6000 buses accommodate 4.5 million passenger journeys on 600 routes around London. Local bus journeys rose in London by 25 per cent between 1991/1992 and 2001/2002 – a period that saw bus use in other British metropolitan areas decline.[31] In central London in 2001, only 12 per cent of people commuted by car, compared to a figure of 41 per cent for the whole of the city.[32] More sprawl equals more car use. Seventy-two per cent of those working in central London used trains, 32 per cent using the Underground and 40 per cent surface rail. Compaction and density encourages public transport use. Men travelled 10.3

miles to work on average in Britain in 1999/2001, 70 per cent further than women (6.1 miles). The average distance between home and work in Britain increased by 17 per cent over ten years from 7.2 miles in 1989/1991 to 8.5 miles in 1999/2001 as cities spread their tentacles outwards.[33] In the EU as a whole between 1975 and 1995 the daily distance travelled per person doubled and a further doubling of traffic is predicted by 2025.[34]

Two contrary trends are occurring in London with regards to transport. On the one hand – and in keeping with expectations of urban sprawl – people are travelling further to work. On the other, London's congestion charge for motor vehicles travelling in central districts has encouraged overland public transport, with fewer people commuting by car and more trips taken on local buses.

The British annual motor vehicle increase is running at 800,000. The movement of freight (measured in tonne kilometres) increased by 42 per cent between 1980 and 2002 and the length of haul of goods moved by road increased by over 40 per cent between 1990 and 2002. This means more traffic delays, given limited space resources, and more congestion, and it costs Britain around £20 billion per year.[35] For the EU as a whole, congestion costs 130 billion euros annually and the total external costs of motorized road traffic are estimated at 270 billion euros per year – around 4 per cent of Europe's gross national product. Calculating all associated car activities into time, the typical American male devotes more than 1600 hours a year to his car, sitting in it while it's moving or stands idling, parking it and searching for it. Add to this the time spent earning the money to pay for it, to meet the monthly instalments, and to pay for petrol, tolls, insurance, taxes and tickets and you arrive at a figure of 66 days or 18.2 per cent of his time.[36] London drivers spend 50 per cent of their time in queues. On average, Londoners spend nine days a year just sitting in a car and just three days walking.[37]

In 1950 there were an estimated 70 million cars, trucks and buses on the world's roads. Towards the end of the century there were between 600 and 700 million. By 2025 the figure is expected to pass 1 billion. Around 15 million vehicles are sold every year in Western Europe alone.[38] When you average the space taken up by small cars and trucks and buses this equates to about 9500km². This is as if just under half the size of Wales were a car park. Put another way, it is the equivalent of back-to-back vehicles stretching on a 1000-lane highway from London to Rome, a 250-lane highway from New York to Moscow, a 120-lane highway stretching from London to Sydney, or a single lane stretching 1.9 million km into space, five times the distance to the moon.[39]

A double-track urban railway can move 30,000 people per hour in each direction. A two-lane road can only handle 3000 to 6000 people an hour in each direction. A double-decker bus carries the same number of people as 20 fully laden cars. A double-decker bus takes up to a seventh of the road space of the equivalent number of cars. Cars need as much road space as five to eight bicycles and as much parking space as 20 bicycles. Buses, coaches and trains in Britain are seven times safer than cars in terms of fatalities per passenger kilometre.[40] But over the past 20 years the overall cost of motoring has in real terms remained at or below the 1980 level while bus fares have risen by 31 per cent and rail fares by 37 per cent.[41]

Materials: Cement, asphalt and steel

In 2000 Londoners consumed 49 million tonnes of materials – 6.7 tonnes per person. Some 27.8 million tonnes were consumed by the construction sector, out of which 26 million tonnes of waste was generated: 15 million by the construction and demolition sectors, 7.9 million by commerce and industry and 3.4 million by households.

Buildings consume some 40 per cent of materials in the global community. And cement is a key component. In 2000 1.56 billion tonnes of Portland cement was manufactured globally. One third of this was produced in China alone.[42] And global demand is expected to double within the next 30 years.

Cement is a noxious, or even obnoxious, substance. Each tonne requires about two tonnes of raw material (limestone and shale), consumes about 4 gigajoules of energy in electricity, process heat and transport (the energy equivalent to 131 m^3 of natural gas), produces its equivalent weight in CO_2, about 3kg of NO_x, a mixture of nitrogen monoxide and nitrogen dioxide that contributes to ground-level smog, and about 0.4 kg of PM_{10}, an airborne particulate matter that is harmful to the respiratory tract when inhaled. Cement manufacturing accounts for approximately 7–8 per cent of CO_2 globally. Yet twice as much concrete is used in construction around the world than the total of all other building materials, including wood, steel, plastic and aluminium.[43] The annual global production of concrete is about 5 billion cubic yards, which is the equivalent of a massive block 1000m long, 1000m wide and 3824m high, a bit higher than Mount Fuji in Japan (3776m).

More than 65,000 square miles of land have been paved in the lower 48 states to accommodate America's 214 million cars; there are 3.9 million miles of roads, enough to circle the Earth at the equator 157 times, in that area alone.[44] This amounts to 2.5 per cent of the total land surface – an area more than the size of Georgia, far, far more if you consider car parks and other areas. For every five cars added to the US fleet, an area the size of a football field is covered with asphalt. Close to half of the land area in most US cities goes to providing roads, highways and parking lots for automobiles, close to two-thirds in the case of Los Angeles. Not many cities calculate their asphalt, but Munich, one of the more environmental cities in Europe, has only 4 per cent pavement, 15 per cent asphalt and 16 per cent built area, against 59 per cent vegetation and 6 per cent bare soils.[45] Of London's 175,000 hectare area, 62 per cent is urban – buildings, asphalt, and pavement – with 30 per cent of London's area dedicated to parkland.[46] Metropolitan Tokyo is 82 per cent covered with asphalt or concrete.[47] An area the size of Leicestershire is now taken up by roads in the UK, with an additional fifth as much land given over to parking. 'Once paved, land is not easily reclaimed,' as environmentalist Rupert Cutler once noted. 'Asphalt is the land's last crop.'[48]

In 1973 the tallest building in the US opened its doors. At 1454 feet tall (110 storeys), the Sears Tower took three years to build at a cost of more than US$150 million. From the Skydeck, on a clear day, you can see four states – Illinois, Indiana, Wisconsin and Michigan. The building contains enough steel to build 50,000 cars, enough telephone wiring to wrap around the world 1.75 times, enough concrete to build an eight-lane, five-mile-long highway; it contains more than 43,000 miles of telephone cable, 2000 miles of electrical wire, 25,000 miles of plumbing and stairways totalling 2232 steps.[49] It took 36,910 tonnes of steel to build the Petronas Towers. The Empire State Building contains 60,000 tonnes of steel – 4500 elephant equivalents – and 10 million bricks.[50] A three-bedroom detached house requires about 10,000 facing bricks. Total brick production in UK is 2.8 billion a year, which if lined up end to end would reach to the moon and back.[51]

The ecological footprint

The ecological footprint is a concept used to calculate the area of land required to meet consumption and waste demands. As well as land and bodies of water required for food, forestry required to absorb carbon dioxide emissions and land used for waste disposal are taken into account. Calculations can be made for any unit of consumption (e.g. the individual) and have been made for the world as a whole, for individual nations and for towns and cities. Unfortunately, there are wide discrepancies in methodologies, making comparisons between cities very difficult: estimates of London's ecological footprint range from 125 to 293 times the size of London itself.[52] Nevertheless, suffice it to say that even at lower estimates, the footprint of London (and that of most cities) extends well beyond its geographical area.

That cities' footprints are far greater than the cities themselves is neither surprising nor necessarily problematic. One would expect an area of dense population to exact disproportionate demands on the planet in terms of area and less peopled regions produce food for ones more so. Agriculture is configured in such a way. However, problems become clear when we look at consumption on a wider scale. For example, Europe's ecological footprint represents an area more than twice the size of the continent. (Americans' needs per capita are nearly twice those of Europeans). And, as a planet, we consume more than the Earth can sustain. Since the early 1980s, we have been living in 'ecological deficit'. In 2001, we used 1.2 times the biocapacity of the Earth.[53]

URBAN LOGISTICS

Putting food on supermarket shelves or supplying the high street with clothes and other consumer durables is no small feat. The guzzling city presents titanic and complex organizational challenges. Sating the demands of a city like London requires the movement of huge ships filled with oil or piled high with minerals or Lego-like containers, thousands of kilometres of pipeline carrying oil and gas, and just-in-time meetings of different transport modes. The port infrastructures of Hong Kong or Rotterdam are small cities in themselves. But since they are usually cut off behind fencing and customs barriers, we often overlook them. Equally, we see trucks on motorways with names like Maersk Sealand or CN, but few of us have much of a grasp of what they are doing.

Logistics is the art and science of coordinating the myriad movements of goods and information within and between nations. It involves the process of strategically and profitably managing the procurement, movement and storage of materials, parts and finished inventory (and the related information flows). City logistics require an intensely complex coordination of tangible and less visible things – trucks, planes and ships on the one hand, computer systems and software on the other. When it works it has the grace of the well-oiled machine, but its resilience is far lower than we think, its fragility exposed in a computer shutdown or traffic crisis. All this may sound dry, but logistics constitutes the respiratory and digestive systems that make cities work; without them cities fall apart.

Logistics is big business. The logistics sector is worth £55 billion to the UK economy alone. It contributes 15–20 per cent of total product costs. The sector currently spans some 63,000 companies, employing 1.7 million people in the UK and, although often neglected, is one of the largest employment sectors in the economy.[54] The size of the US logistics industry is US$900 billion – almost double the size of the high-tech industry, or more than 10 per cent of US gross domestic product.[55] The global logistics industry is worth US$3.43 trillion.[56] This includes a wide variety of jobs, from vehicle tracking, cargo securing and protection to customs brokerage, warehousing, distribution and the associated IT connected to these activities.

And it is a fast growing business. Food imports and exports have tripled over 20 years in the UK.[57] Significantly, recent years have seen the emergence of third party logistics companies (3PLs) who are solely concerned with organizing these movements. Theoretically, and historically, there are a number of different players in the supply chain whose activities have to be coordinated: road haulers, rail operators, shipping companies, airlines, freight forwarders, warehousing companies, postal companies, and packaging and distribution companies. Increasingly, however, sophisticated one-stop companies – 3PLs with unfamiliar names like Christian Salvesen, Wincanton, and Tibbet & Britten – offer solutions over a range of sectors. New software and satellite technology tracks inventory and movement, allowing suppliers and importers to locate their shipment at any one time. The newest trend is radio frequency identification (RFID), which is now being standardized at a global level, allowing companies to tag all their goods to provide uninterrupted tracking of goods in transit.

Sea ports are the main hubs of global freight distribution. There are some 2000 ports worldwide, from single-berth operations handling a few hundred tonnes a year to multipurpose facilities handling up to 300 million tonnes a year. The largest include Shanghai, Singapore, Hong Kong, New York, Houston, Rotterdam, Hamburg and the ports around Tokyo Bay. Fewer and fewer ports handle the lion's share of world traffic: the top ten container ports handle close to 40 per cent of world traffic today. You can recognize the containers in any port: Maersk Line (with 18 per cent of world trade, by far the largest), Mediterranean Shipping Co., Evergreen from Taiwan, Cosco (China Ocean Shipping) from Beijing, Hanjin from Seoul and NYK Line from Tokyo.

Port infrastructures can be massive. For example, Rotterdam's Europort stretches 40km and covers 10,500 hectares (industrial sites plus water), has 60,600 people in directly port-related employment and handles some 1 million tonnes of goods every day. In 2005 the equivalent of 8 million 20-foot containers passed through Rotterdam. The port is now expanding by claiming land from the sea.

World port traffic surpassed 5 billion tonnes in 1998 and it is estimated that by 2010 world seaborne freight will approach 7 billion tonnes. Of this, Chinese ports will handle about 4 billion tonnes of freight throughput, 57 per cent of the total.[58] Forty-five per cent of sea freight is liquid. Dry bulk goods – coal, iron ore, grain, phosphate – make up 23 per cent and general cargo accounts for the remaining 32 per cent. The transportation of general cargo has become increasingly containerized. Freight containers are typically 20 feet long, 8 feet wide, and, usually, a little over 8 feet high. Some are 40 feet long. One twenty foot equivalent unit (TEU) equals about 12 register tonnes or 34m^3. One TEU can carry 2200 VCRs or 5000 pairs of shoes. There are estimated to be 15.9 million TEU containers in the world. Container traffic breaks down globally thus: the Far East 45 per cent, Europe 23 per cent, North America 16 per cent, the Near and Middle East 6 per cent, Central and South America 4 per cent and Africa 3 per cent. Movements of empty containers are estimated to make up about 20 per cent of the total. In 2003 sea port container traffic was 266.3 million TEUs, treble the container traffic in 1990. Thus more goods are moving around faster.

Ports handle about 26,500 ships of over 500 gross tonnage criss-crossing the seas. They include 5500 crude oil tankers and oil product tankers, which between them can carry 175 million tonnes of oil, 2600 container ships, 4900 bulk carriers carrying loads such as grains, over 2000 chemical tankers and around 11,500 general cargo ships sailing around the world. The largest ports handle the super-sized ships, over 300m long, that can carry up to 9000 20-foot containers, 13 storeys high and 10 containers wide. One of the largest, the OOCL Shenzhen, can carry up to 100,000 tonnes of cargo; it is driven by a single 12-cylinder, 69,439kW (93,120bhp) engine which turns an 85 tonne propeller. By way of comparison, a typical family car engine generates around 90kW (120hp), 776 times less. Fuel consumption is measured in tonnes of fuel consumed per hour, and the rate is around 10 tonnes. On the drawing board is the MalaccaMax ship, 470m long, 60m high, with 16 storeys, an 18,000 container capacity and a 200,000 tonne cargo capacity.[59]

Has decivilization started?

We live in awkward times. Between now and 2050 world population is expected to grow by 50 per cent and, as we have seen, our per capita consumptive demands on the planet are also growing fast. In the 1960s the world's ecological footprint was below the planet's biocapacity; by the end of the 1970s it had risen to about one planet, where it stayed until about 1983. By the end of the millennium our footprint had reached 1.2 planets. We have now been living in ecological deficit for two decades.[60] At the same time, wealth differentials are getting more extreme. Global inequality is worse than it has ever been. Such trends gloomily raise the question, Has modernity failed us? Has, indeed, decivilization already begun?

In 1992 Francis Fukuyama buoyantly declared in his book *The End of History and the Last Man* that the end of the Cold War meant the end of the progression of human history with Western liberal democracy as the triumphant, final form of human government and liberal economics as the ultimately prevailing mode of production. However, this thesis has not been able to withstand geopolitical – Balkanization, Islamic fundamentalism – and environmental objections. Capitalist ideologies assume inexhaustible resources which just aren't there. The global economy cannot, or

Source: Charles Landry

The basic infrastructures of life simply do not exist in many places across the world – such as Shkodra, Albania (above)

plain won't, continue in its present form. We cannot rely on the market to respond appropriately to environmental, social and cultural crises in time because environmental, social and cultural costs are not factored into economic calculations.

Barring manna from heaven or an extraordinary scientific discovery, it is safe to say that civilization will not survive in its present form. This is not to make an ideological point. There's just not enough planet to maintain culture as we now know it. Our addiction to the automobile will have to be addressed because even if or when sustainable energy sources arrive on a widespread, global scale, we do not have an infinite supply of metal. Tastes will change as we readjust to agricultures and industries closer to home. Water will become, as it should be, precious.

Given this material backdrop, ideologies will of course change. Perhaps the current rhetoric of rational economic man will be seen retrospectively as rather mad. The cult of individualism may wane when we realize in full how dependent our individual existences are on others (since we are all in effect sharing the same pie, having more means someone else having less). And change will be traumatic. Extreme economic crisis has historically precipitated extreme ideologies.

THE GEOGRAPHY OF MISERY

Light and shade accompany the urban story, and in some places it is the dark that dominates. Too often, grinding poverty, hopelessness, drug dealing, child prostitution, people-trafficking, petty crime, street children, AIDS and the fear induced by local gangs characterize the urban experience. And let's not forget Grozny or Baghdad. We can take extremes of suffering and well-being as a given. Columbia's murder rate is 100 times that of Copenhagen. Gloom is fairly unavoidable when you dwell on these thoughts, and trying to empathize with the city's most afflicted hurts in the gut.

But misery is exactly where the greater focus of creativity should be. Forget for the moment the more attractive glamour of new media industries or the latest icon building in a city centre. Finding imaginative solutions to day-to-day needs, human distress, thwarted ambition, and crime and violence is a far more creative act. The creativity needed has different qualities. Good ideas are interwoven with courage, the skill of mediation, negotiation, dialogue and even love.

This chapter and the two that follow approach the concept of geography in terms of the way feelings and experiences are distributed over physical space. Further, these chapters explore how misery, desire or mere blandness can pervade the way a city looks and *feels*. Endemic misery among an urban population, for instance, will impact on the subjective experience of a visitor to their city. But misery may also be reflected in the physical structure of the city: crumbling buildings, filthy streets, public spaces no longer tended by a local authority, no-go areas. And the same applies to desire and blandness, which can manifest themselves in advertising clutter or homogenized shopping malls respectively.

Misery exists everywhere, even in our most affluent cities – mundane, everyday miseries of redundancy, not being able to make ends meet or the alienation that dense but fragmented communities can induce. However, I concentrate here on extremes of misery to illustrate more starkly how creativity can be brought to bear on problems we are all too aware of, if probably not close to.

While sometimes grim, these narratives are intended to emphasize hope rather than despair. Even for a city in acute distress, those that live there can still harbour a love. In each of the cities mentioned in the pages that follow, there are wonderful people battling against the odds. As we survey misery, consider the NGO Viva Rio's campaign 'Choose Gun Free! It's Your Weapon or Me', where women are taking the lead in reducing debilitating levels of gun violence in the favelas. Consider Viktor Melnikov, the surprise new mayor of shockingly polluted Norilsk, who is trying to force the local mining company into safer practices. Consider the project that Cirque du Soleil, in conjunction with Save the Children, and in addition to its shelters, has developed to provide circus training as an alternative to education for the street children who lived in the sewers and heating pipes beneath the streets of Ulan Bator.

Or consider the reaction 'without precedent in Japanese society'[61] to the Kobe earthquake of 1995, which killed 6279 people. Although volunteerism is not nearly as widespread in Japan as in Europe or North America, most search and rescue was undertaken by community residents. Spontaneous volunteering and emergent group activity were widespread throughout the emergency period. Residents provided a wide range of goods and services to their fellow earthquake victims, and large numbers of people travelled from other parts of the country to offer aid. Officially designated rescue agencies such as fire departments and civil defence forces were responsible for recovering at most one quarter of those trapped in collapsed structures. There was not a single authenticated case of looting.[62]

To focus on misery can depress, yet it provides a broad and rich context in which to imagine positive, original alternatives. A reminder of urban difficulties challenges us to imagine deep down what it is really like to live in such places. It reminds us what the challenge is to creativity: to build civility, a civic culture and some sense of fairness, to curtail the corrupt, to generate jobs, and to create cities that can do more than just serve basic needs.

Organized crime and the rule of fear

For centuries now the Italian Mafia has distorted and impoverished the South Italian economy, extorting shopkeepers and taking a cut on any economic activity. Even today it seems it takes a cut on any big construction project. This is why Rico Cassone, the mayor of Villa San Giovanni who opposed building the Messina Bridge to connect Sicily to the mainland, resigned – he received the classic Mafia threat of five bullets through the post. Organized crime is expected to profit hugely from the bridge's construction. But their tentacles go much further. Building cities is a construction game, so Mafia involvement in Southern Italian city-making will continue *ad nauseam*.

The yakuza in Japan, like other mobster groups, are far more than gangs of thugs that oversee extortion, gambling, prostitution and other traditional gangster activities. They have bought up real estate and have their tentacles in some 900 construction-related firms. The three largest groups are the Kobe-based Yamaguchi-gumi and the Sumiyoshi-Rengo-kai and Inagawa-kai, both headquartered in Tokyo. The National Police Agency indicated that the Yamaguchi-gumi had 20,826 members and 737 affiliated groups in the late 1990s.[63] In 1998 the *South China Morning Post* reported Japanese police data on mob involvement in the nation's construction industry, showing that Japan's mobsters stood to make about US$9 billion just in the reconstruction needed after the major earthquake hit the port city of Kobe in 1995. The same story is repeated with the Chinese triads in Taiwan, Macau and the wider diaspora. It is evident also in places like Moscow, where older tenants are brutalized out of their cheap communist tenancies in desirable areas to make way for new construction and where listed buildings are burnt down to enable new building at higher plot ratios. And the US mafia's historic involvement in construction is well documented.

Think of Belfast, where a number of the 'freedom fighters' on both sides of the religious divide – Catholic and Protestant – now hold whole communities to ransom as they slide into drug dealing, racketeering and violence under the guise of protecting their communities. Think too of the apartheid on the ground that still continues in spite of efforts towards peace. Like a poison, it leaches into the daily fabric of life. For instance, in the Ardoyne district of Belfast, four out of every five Protestant residents will not use the nearest shops because they are located in Catholic streets, and a similar proportion of Catholics will not swim in their nearest swimming pool, which is located in a Protestant street. Most 18-year-olds in Ardoyne have never in their life had a meaningful conversation, about, say, sport or family, with anybody of their own age across the 'peace line' and religious divide.[64] The connection between segregation and deprivation is startling. Virtually all the most deprived areas are highly segregated and have the most significant levels of sectarian violence. The link between economic well-being and prejudice is clear.[65]

Rio conjures up a particularly powerful resonance: carnival, dance, gyrating, big-busted girls, Copacabana beach and the Sugarloaf. But any party atmosphere is severely compromised by the threat of gangs. Drug organizations like Red Command control most of the city's 26 sprawling shanty towns or favelas, whose population exceeds a couple of million people. The leader of the Red Command drug organization, Luiz Fernando da Costa, better known as Fernandinho Beira Mar, has been in a top-security prison since 2001, but he still exerts power. He is reputed to have negotiated arms deals on his mobile phone there. In 2002 he managed to torture, murder and burn four of his enemies. To murder his opponents he needed the connivance of prison staff to be able to move through six sets of iron gates. Prison staff are threatened if they do not accept bribes. The repercussions reached Rio. Armed supporters of one of Mar's victims, Ernaldo Pinto de Medeiros, moved slowly from street to street ordering shops to close and schools to send their children home as a mark of respect. Rio, normally chaotic, fell silent.

Rio's largest favela, Rocinha, prone to landslides as it clings to the hillside above high-class beachside areas which provide easy access employment for residents, is often held up as an example of a greatly improved area of squatter housing. However, pitched battles between the police and drug lords have drawn attention to its underlying social problems and the challenges that still lie ahead for city planners. The sheer size, topographical complexity and social structures of Rio's favelas mean that police are reluctant to intervene unless serious violence or drug-trafficking has been detected. Rocinha is in fact the largest favela in South America, with some 127,000 residents. Despite a more violent past, it is now relatively peaceful – thousands of tourists even visit each year, often on organized tours. Yet Rio is a major transit point for Colombian cocaine on its way to Europe and represents a big market itself for the drug. Higher up the hill, in a community that is both socially and spatially segmented, lie parts of Rocinha that are largely controlled by drug lords, not the city authorities. But lower down there is a structure of local government and the community has developed services for itself, such as crèches, and three-quarters of residents now have access to electricity. The 2002 film *City of God* shone a spotlight on favelas, chronicling the cycle of poverty, violence, and despair in a Rio de Janeiro slum.

Overall the murder rate in metro Rio is declining. It is now 50 per 100,000 inhabitants per annum, down from 78 in 1994, although in some favelas like Baixada Fluminense the murder rate is still 76. But it is not only murder that shifts perceptions. 'Gunmen rob British coach party in Rio – Raiders storm airport bus carrying 33 elderly British tourists – cameras and jewellery worth thousands snatched,' read a headline earlier this year.[66] The road that links Rio's international airport to the glitzy South Zone has become notorious in recent years for carjackings and shootings. In Rio they speak of the 'parallel power' that traffickers exert while enriching themselves, or even of a 'parallel state'.

Gary, Indiana, with a population of 120,000, has a murder rate of 79 per 100,000, the highest in the US. Dominated by drug gangs fighting for turf, it is a hollowed out, desolated place and has been so for a couple of decades. The drug dealing is seductive – you can triple your money turning cocaine into crack and if you are very lucky move on when you have some money. But most end up dead or in prison. In 1995, when the murder rate was 118, the state governor ordered in the state troopers amid great fanfare. On national TV he ordered them to go to war on Gary's gangs. The troopers set up roadblocks in the most dangerous neighbourhoods. During their three-month stay the murder rate went down by 40 per cent only to go back up again when they left. Once a racially mixed steel town, a dozen years after the mills began to shrink from employing 30,000 workers in the 1970s, it became a wretched black ghetto. Today employment hovers at around 5000.

The story of Gary's descent into violence is an extreme version of one played out in many American cities where 'white flight' is followed by 'urban blight'. But murder rates are only one indication of urban distress. Behind these murders lie untold stories of violence, unpleasantness, paranoia and fear. One may note that the average murder rate in the US is 5.6 per 100,000 people, with New Orleans on 53.3, Washington on 45.8 and New York, with its dramatic reduction in crime, on 7.3. Contrast this with two of the most multicultural cities in the world, Toronto on 1.80 and Vancouver on 3.45.

People-trafficking and the sex trade

After drugs and arms trading, the £4 billion global sex trade business comes in third in illegal trade. An estimated 600,000–800,000 people are trafficked in this way per annum, according to the US State Department. I witnessed for myself several instances in Iasi in Romania on the Moldavian border and then in Moldova's capital Kishinev: burly, blurry-eyed men in their 40s shacked up in hotels with waif-like 18-year-olds waiting to be transported on. The contrasts in Kishinev are stark. The main thoroughfares have some faded class and a mix of garish bars, clubs and shrill advertising. In the evening, you see hoards of scantily dressed young women, the target of the traffickers. Immediately off the main roads there is no street lighting and you are enveloped in gloom. The European Parliament estimates that around 4000 women a year are trafficked to Denmark and over 10,000 to the UK. Many come from Eastern Europe but others increasingly from places like Thailand, Nigeria and Sierra Leone. Often they are sold on to work as prostitutes who can make several thousand pounds a week for their pimps and are effectively imprisoned in our major cities. The London Metropolitan Police estimate some are forced to see between 30 and 40 clients per day. It is estimated that only 19 per cent of prostitutes in

London are British: 25 per cent are Eastern Europeans and 13 per cent are of Southeast Asian origin.

Pattya, 100 miles east of Bangkok, where the streets are lined with go-go bars and where English-style pubs display signs declaring 'lager louts welcome', teems with prostitutes. Of the 200,000 inhabitants, it is estimated that 100,000 have some kind of connection to sex tourism. Pattya's population virtually doubles during the winter months, when affluent European and American tourists – many of them well past middle age – flee the cold of their own countries to seek the warm weather and sensual pleasures of Pattya. Three decades ago, Pattya was an obscure fishing village. With the advent of the Vietnam War, it became a popular recreation resort for American marines based at nearby Sattaship; their weekend escapades sowed the seeds of the sex industry. From that beginning, prostitution spread like wildfire. Because of the enormous financial success of sex tourism, thousands of young women and girls barely into their teens come from the impoverished villages of northern Thailand to seek the easy money. Even women and girls from neighbouring Myanmar, Cambodia and Vietnam are brought to work in the sex shops. And lurking behind the lure of pleasure lies endless violence.

Cambodia has become a favoured destination for paedophiles since Thailand, previously the most notorious centre of under-age sex, began a crackdown on child prostitution two years ago. The paedophiles come from America, Canada, Australia, Holland and Germany, as well as Britain. Svay Pak, the infamous brothel area 11km north of central Phnom Penh, is the epicentre. 'Out here you can get anything, you do what the fuck you like, girl, boy, two-year-old baby, whatever you want. Nobody cares.'[67] And Pattya and Svay Pak are just at the apex of many more towns and cities across the region that rely on sex and have lost their dignity.

The human cost of change

Over the South China Sea to Port Moresby, the capital of Papua New Guinea. No other country has been wrenched into the modern world with such brutal swiftness, and it is now on the brink of social and economic meltdown. For two years running it came out worst in the Economist Intelligence Unit's liveability rankings of 130 cities, behind the likes of Lagos, Algiers and Karachi.[68] Crime is extremely high, armed hold-ups perpetuated by *raskols* are common, and expatriates and middle-class locals live behind high walls and coils of razor wire. Yet grass-roots crime may simply reflect the corruption of authority: '*Raskols* mimic political leaders' corrupt behaviour at the street level, enriching themselves through theft and operating with relative impunity. When criminals and corrupt politicians go unpunished, people lose respect for state laws and the authority of central government collapses.'[69]

Back North. While admiring the amazing growth and sparkle of the new China, let us not forget the grim cost of China's economic miracle, even though in comparison with other recently developing countries in the region, this immense logistical challenge has been managed with some sense of planning and order. There are only a few slums, a significant achievement given that this is the biggest mass migration in the history of the world, with rural people move into cities creating a second industrial revolution. A massive building boom, unparalleled anywhere, is taking place. In 2003 half of the concrete used in construction around the world was used in China's cities. In 1950, 72 million Chinese lived in cities; in 1997 the figure was 370 million and by 2020 it is predicted to be 800 million, perhaps 950 million by 2030. The extreme example is Shenzhen, constructed at breakneck speed by 'architects on acid'.[70] In the 1970s it was a fishing village. Then the government established a special economic zone there and the growth was non-stop. Recent government estimates put the population at 10 million, well above the 7 million counted in the 2000 census. We hear little about the industrial and construction accidents of this expansion. Official estimates are that 11,000 are killed every year, but it is privately acknowledged to be more than 20,000 a year.[71] China competes on price in the global market and safety measures add costs to the bottom line. This speed of development means safety standards do not catch up and compensation is so low there is little incentive for operators to ensure safety.

Furthermore, in spite of increased awareness of pollution, the environmental crisis appears in danger of getting out of control. China's spectacular economic growth over the past two decades has dramatically depleted the country's natural resources and produced skyrocketing rates of pollution. Environmental degradation has also contributed to significant public health problems, mass migration, economic loss and social unrest. 'The result is a patchwork of environmental protection in which a few wealthy regions with strong leaders and international ties improve their local conditions, while most of the country continues to deteriorate.' Elizabeth C. Economy documents in a gripping way the severely degraded environment where 'rivers run black, deserts advance from the north and smoky haze covers the country'.[72]

Imagine, after a hard day's work, being cocooned in small apartments in endlessly similar 25-storey blocks in ever-burgeoning cities. Think of the social life, leisure, shopping. And yet 'It is better living here than living in my home village in Anhui,' comments a Beijing resident.[73]

Grinding poverty and stolen childhood

> *The suffocation, by surveillance, shadowing, wiretapping and mail interception, is total. Most patients in hospitals suffer from psychosomatic illnesses, worn out by compulsory drills, innumerable parades, 'patriotic' assemblies at six in the morning and droning propaganda. They are toil-worn, prostrate, at the end of their tether. Clinical depression is rampant. Alcoholism is common because of mind-numbing rigidities, regimentation and hopelessness. In patients' eyes I saw no life, only lassitude and a constant fear.[74]*

North Korea represents a 'prison state' where criticism of the state constitutes treason. Pyongyang recoils from outside intervention, but recent appeals for aid reveal the desperation of a people shut off from the rest of the world. In fact, in relative terms, the capital is a better place to live than the countryside and its residents would find the idea of Western middle classes *wanting* to move out of the city quite bizarre. Pyongyang's restaurants and nightclubs contrast absolutely with rural North Korea, where citizens face crippling poverty, with starvation particularly rampant among children. But repression also takes its toll on childhood:

> *Children have had the creativity and spontaneity of childhood taken away from them. The unquestioning following of the instructions and behaviour of adults suggest that the children are aware of the consequences of misbehaviour in adulthood and don't wish to dabble in it. There is a sense of defeat about children's behaviour – that they are subconsciously aware of the intransigence of the status quo and have decided to meekly accept it.[75]*

Meanwhile, in Mongolia's capital, Ulan Bator, where temperatures can fall as low as -52°C in winter, more than 3000 children live on the streets. Many shelter in the sewers for warmth, refuge and to escape violence in the city. The collapse of communism saw most factories shutting down, leaving thousands unemployed. The result was escalating crime, domestic violence and alcoholism. This poverty forced children out of their homes and now they beg, steal and wander the ice-covered streets.[76]

Filth

Let's explore some of Russia's (and the world's) most polluted cities, such as Norilsk, 2875km east of Moscow, in Siberia, at the edge of the Arctic circle, where the temperatures can drop to -60°C in winter, Dzerzhinsk about 380km further east, or Murmansk and the Kola Peninsula. In Norilsk the snow turns black, and is discoloured yellow across a 30km radius, and the air tastes sour from sulphurous fumes. It is a closed city, but one which my Comedia colleague Phil Wood had the pleasure to visit. Like 90 other towns and cities, it is normally off-limits to foreigners. The authorities say that this restriction is to protect Norilsk from Azerbaijani traders flocking to this economic zone. Others argue it has more to do with hiding highly unpleasant facts. A former Soviet penal colony, safety was never a concern. Norilsk, with a population of 230,000, is home to the world's biggest nickel mine and known for industrial pollution so severe it drifts over to Canada. Evidence of Norilsk's activities has also been found on polar ice. The city itself is a paradise compared to what goes on in the plants, where workers wear respirators as fumes giddy the senses and where 'workers' lives have, over several decades, been remorselessly put upon the sacrificial block'.[77] Chimney stacks to the south, east, north and west mean the city is hit by pollution whatever way the wind blows. The appalling conditions mean the average life expectancy is ten years below the Russian average and the men in the mines live barely beyond 50. Norilsk produces 14.5 per cent of all factory pollution in Russia,[78] an astonishing fact given Russia's poor pollution record. Each day the stacks blurt out 5000 tonnes of sulphur dioxides into the sky. The lure, however, is the high wages.

Source: Charles Landry

One of around 600,000 bunkers in Albania:
these are often in the most unlikely urban settings, built
under Enver Hoxha's leadership to control the population

Prisons and borders

Think of the once-proud Shkodra in Albania, now forgotten at the edge of Montenegro, where electricity is still intermittent and the potholes are deep enough to conceal a small child. The population was transformed after the flight of many of the ambitious to Tirana, tempted by its glitz and apparent opportunities. The mountain villagers, who in turn are tempted by Shkodra, have replaced them. Clannish attitudes linger in the city and family blood feuds persist. For instance, in December 2000 the nephew of Ndoc Cefa, a famous Albanian theatre director, assassinated another Albanian in London. While the assassin is locked up in a psychiatric hospital in Albania, the blood feud must continue and all males of the Cefa family in the Shkodra area are targets. Their houses are their prisons.

Consider the wall separating Israel from the West Bank and partly running through Palestinian territory. It was built to prevent Palestinian would-be suicide bombers from entering Israel. It is part wall, part fence, and most of its 670km length has a concrete base and a 5m-high wire-and-mesh superstructure. Rolls of razor wire and a 4m-deep ditch are placed on one side. In addition, the structure is fitted with electronic sensors and it has an earth-covered 'trace road' beside it where footprints of anyone crossing can be seen. Parts of the structure consist of an 8m-high solid concrete wall, complete with massive watchtowers. Many towns are cut off or cut up by the wall. Imagine living in Qalqilya, where the wall surrounds the town almost completely. Residents are imprisoned, cut off from neighbouring Palestinian villages and the rest of the West Bank. Palestinian property within 35m of the wall, including homes, farms, agricultural land, greenhouses and water wells, has been destroyed by the Israeli army. Four entrances to the town have been blocked, while the only remaining entrance is a military roadblock. It denies locals the means to livelihood and access to natural resources. Qalqilya was once known as the West Bank's bread basket, but nearly 50 per cent of the city's agricultural land has been confiscated, as have 19 wells, representing 30 per cent of the city's water supply, forcing residents to migrate to sustain a livelihood.[79]

Border towns, especially between countries where wealth differentials are great, can also be problematic. Cuidad Juarez in Mexico and El Paso, Texas effectively constitute one city but they are separated by the Rio Grande River and the border. More than 320 women have been murdered in Juarez since 1993. Of these deaths, approximately 100 have been sexual-torture killings of young women aged between 12 and 19. Several hundred women are missing and unaccounted for. Nobody takes responsibility for solving the cases and corrupt police are in cahoots with the public prosecutor's office. The powerful drug cartels and outdated laws have allowed the perpetrators to go free. Since 1995 police have jailed more than a dozen killers but the murder spree continues and has now attracted global attention, with Amnesty International at the campaigning forefront.

Tourism and its discontents

What about the gleaming tourist spots of Faliraki, Goa or Ibiza? Thousands of places worldwide are caught up in the tourism maelstrom, and, while it has clearly done much for many places, it also has its flip side: the effect on local identity, ecological despoliation, overdevelopment and more. Fuelled by cheap airlines, charter flights and media attention, Faliraki, the once sleepy fishing village on Rhodes, became a 'modern-day Sodom', according to some, after a TV series called *Club Reps*, which followed the activities of holidaymakers and reps. It rapidly became a destination for British youngsters and developed into a place of binge drinking orgies, fighting, vomiting and casual sex, encouraged, it must be said, by local bar owners. In 2004 it had clubs with names like Sinners, Excite, Bed, Climax and The Pleasure Rooms. Then the authorities clamped down after a fatal stabbing of a British boy in a drunken brawl and introduced a zero tolerance policy. Quickly the action moved on to Zakynthos. Once exclusive, for the moment it enjoys the dubious reputation of being the party haven of Europe. But in the evening a darker side quickly emerges. Barely dressed girls weave their way drunkenly between guys whose strut has been reduced to an alcoholic crawl. Flashes of violence and casual sex skirt the streets and rape is then never far away.

Goa, once a dope-filled, peace-loving haven, has long lost its innocent, fun-loving reputation, blown away by a spate of drug deaths as the hippie paradise is taken over by British traffickers. Ibiza, once a Spanish idyll, is now another party haven invaded by unshackled tourists. The club names are again appropriate: Amnesia, Eden, El Divino.

Cultural prosperity among poverty

As I have already suggested, acute misery is not confined to developing nations. Material poverty exists alongside prosperity. Nevertheless, culture can be wielded to alleviate poverty by recentring communities and by providing a foundation upon which tangible, material economies can be built.

Paris' Val-Fourre sink estate is Europe's largest council estate, with 28,000 inhabitants, sky-high unemployment and growing school drop rates – inevitably worse for the immigrants, most of whom are from North Africa. Despite the republican French ideal of equality, they do not feel treated and respected as French. The combination – no job, no education, no respect – is a dangerous cocktail as the riots in the *banlieues* all over France in late 2005 showed. But here, as in so many other places, there are bright sparks such as *Radio Droit de Cite*, run by 60 local teenagers. The station gives them a platform on which to shape their identity and foster self-belief through producing documentaries, phone-ins, community information, sports and music. More than a dozen teenagers from the station have moved on to jobs in national broadcasting.

Finally, back to my home country, Britain, where the Joseph Rowntree Foundation revealed that 70 per cent of Britain's poorest children are concentrated in just four conurbations: London, Greater Manchester, Merseyside (which includes Liverpool) and Glasgow.[80] The Rowntree report points out 'the huge damage caused by the persistence of poverty and disadvantage in a generally prosperous country'. The poor areas in these cities, like Harpurhey in Manchester, Everton in Liverpool, Tower Hamlets in London or Easterhouse in Glasgow, can feel like desolated places, but here, as elsewhere, civic leadership can produce innovative ideas. For example, in Easterhouse a new Cultural Campus, appropriately called the Bridge, has opened, incorporating a library, a lifelong learning centre, a flexible auditorium, rehearsal, photography and multimedia studios, a flexible exhibition and performance space, and an education centre, the John Wheatley College. This large, multifunctional building also offers office suites, a new swimming pool, water features and a health suite, which will attract many users. Its goals are to increase opportunities to develop personal self-confidence, new life skills, such as communication and team working, and good health and to increase employability. Most interestingly and counter-intuitively, it is also the base for the new National Theatre of Scotland. Conceived as a 'virtual' body, with only a small number of permanent staff, it will research at the Easterhouse base and create plays for touring. This alone will bring people into the area who previously had no reason to be there.

In London the new Idea Stores in Tower Hamlets are remodelling the view of libraries, which were previously underused and unloved. The plan is to create a series of bright, new buildings in local shopping areas, combining lifelong learning and cultural attractions with all the services normally associated with libraries, from classic books to DVDs and CDs. They borrow the best that can be learnt from the world of retail – presentation, use of colour, sense of welcome – while retaining a public service ethos. The first three in Bow, Chrisp Street and Whitechapel have an airy, transparent feel, in tune with a democratic spirit and that of valuing users as citizens. The first Idea Stores have trebled the number of visitors. The dowdiness of the old libraries has been left behind and a new image has drawn in new users. Acting as a community hub, the word library has disappeared. We now have Idea Stores, complete with cafés, crèches and multimedia offerings. Whether the word 'store' reflects the right ethos is another matter.

The Easterhouse Cultural Campus and Tower Hamlets' Ideas Stores projects attempt to build social capital, characterized by encouraging social trust and mutual interconnectedness, which is enhanced over time though interaction. The analogy with capital can be misleading, because unlike traditional forms of capital, social capital is not depleted by use, but in fact grows by use and is depleted by non-use. It is accumulated when people interact in a purposeful manner with each other in families, workplaces, neighbourhoods, local associations and other meeting places.

Learning from Katha

The goal of the art of city-making is to create more liveable places with decent services, good housing and the possibility of a livelihood. If these are missing, not to mention the basics like shelter, food, drinkable water and elementary security, there is the danger of falling back into chaos in spite of the selfless and courageous acts of individuals.

I want to conclude the geography of misery with the story of an organization I know well. It stands as an exemplar for all the other creative projects around the world that attempt to grapple with ordinary and dramatic misery in cities. It reminds us how the worst can be turned into something better.

It is called Katha and it works largely in Delhi's largest slum, Govindpuri, where 150,000 people live. Katha is now at the epicentre of activities that are transforming the Govindpuri slum cluster. Katha supports people's movements in over 54 communities with the aim of turning 'the slums into the gold mines they are – the powerhouses of creativity, entrepreneurship and drive'. Its slogan is 'uncommon creativities for a common good' based on an 'uncommon education' (visit www.katha.org for more information).

The word *katha* itself means story or narrative. It started with a simple idea 'to enhance the joy of reading' and to foster storytelling. India has always been a land of storytellers. It honed over centuries the fine art of telling the story – in epics, mythologies, folk tales and more recent writings. Stories can transmit values, morals and culture. Founded in 1988 by Geeta Dharmarajan, Katha started as a small publishing house translating stories from the different Indian regions. But the story idea has had greater impact. The organization then started schools and income generation projects in Govindpuri.

Its educational ethos is centred on developing a story each term. There are no discrete topics such as biology or maths. Children learn these through the story along the way. I was involved when the theme was 'Transforming the City, Urban Stories'. In its main school and 12 smaller ones the whole curriculum was focused on the city and all the rooms had city themes. They surveyed sewage conditions in their own slum and so learnt about safe water, biological processes, bacteria and diseases. In bringing together the results they grasped proportions, percentages and statistics and so got to know maths. By interviewing residents and writing up impressions, they learnt to articulate and craft language and learnt how to create presentations on computers. By building models of how their slum can develop, they learn how to design, paint and make models. And they get to know their community: every day their urban story gets added to through talking to their parents, friends and neighbours.

Since the Katha schools started in the early 1990s, over 6000 children have benefited and over 1000 have gone on to higher education, this in an area when illiteracy runs very high. But in order to get parents interested in sending their children to school, Katha started a women's entrepreneurship programme, which in 1995 evolved into the Katha School of Entrepreneurship, to develop leadership, mentoring and work. The idea of '[SHE][2]' is at its core, meaning that any investment in women brings double the results.[81] Hundreds of women in the last decade have gone out into the community and entered full-time employment as home helps or office workers or started businesses as stallholders or tailors earning up to 20 times what they did before. Many have gone on to take further education courses. There is an in-house bakery at Katha that employs some of Katha's beneficiaries. This education and employment provides women with resources with which to send their children to Katha schools. Parents pay a small but, for a slum dweller, significant fee (£4 a year) – Katha believes this personal investment increases commitment and motivation. Yet it is possible to recoup all the fees through results attendance and the involvement of parents in schooling. Additional costs (£50 per year per pupil) are obtained from grants and sponsorship.

Katha has now added city development to its repertoire. Again, its ethos here is poor-friendly, taking the ideas and aspirations of the impoverished into consideration. It asks them how they want to improve their environment and to bring themselves decent lifestyles. It seeks equitable growth, with more people involvement, as only then will growth be viable or sustainable. From 2007 onwards Katha will begin to help redevelop a part of Govindpuri through a process of co-designing and co-creation with the local community.

The Katha philosophy has grown organically over the years, yet at its core is a desire to stimulate an interest in lifelong learning that will help children grow into confident, self-reliant, responsible and responsive adults; to build social capital; to empower; to help break down gender, cultural and social stereotypes; and to encourage everyone to foster excellence and expand their creativity.

Katha's '9 Cs' slogan, based on what they believe helps form character, is embellished on a main column in the principal school. It could stand for what *The Art of City-Making* is attempting to promote:

Curiosity	Competence	Concern
Creativity	Confidence	Cooperation
Critical Thinking	Concentration	Citizenship

THE GEOGRAPHY OF DESIRE

Desire is the flip side of misery. Let's look again at Rio de Janeiro, where desire and misery clash. The city has a powerful resonance: sexuality, heat, glamour, energy. Our vantage point is the giant 38m-high Christ the Redeemer statue on the Corcovado mountain, 710m above sea level. The city's vista is unrivalled anywhere in the world, even by Sydney, San Francisco, Hong Kong or Vancouver. Even the favelas look enticing. But down on the ground, things are different. The 1950s and 1960s, as nearly everywhere, took their toll, as rampant redevelopment fractured the tree-lined boulevards and decorative apartments.

Carnival, beautiful women and men, samba, bossa nova. Even the once seedy and dangerous Lapa is now a hub of the music scene and is a regenerator's dream: faded 19th century houses and warehouses are waiting to be turned into more hip apartments and offices. It still has an edginess, yet the clubs, bars and restaurants are opening and beginning to tame the threats.

Rio's resonance is why the Guggenheim wants to be linked with it. The associational richness of the two brands, Rio and Guggenheim, seems irresistible; they are a city-marketer's dream. At first, the idea was to help regenerate the Mauá Pier area in the historic centre of Rio de Janeiro. The redevelopment of this site as a new cultural centre is expected to be a crucial and strategic land-mark in Rio's plans to bring life back to the Cais do Porto region. Apparently mutually beneficial, the aim of redevelopment is to strengthen the Guggenheim's 'global brand' and turn Rio into a 'global city'. Visionary architecture was contractually required, and Jean Nouvel was chosen and has provided the design.

But there has been a stand-off: The plan has stalled politically and the city cannot get it approved. The battle lines are drawn between those who believe the Guggenheim will be a regenerator and those who think it will only gentrify the area and be of little or no benefit to the poor. The fate of the Rio/Guggenheim connection is the supreme symbol of *The Art of City-Making* story and of the battle of how to deal with misery. Do you create fashionable desire, whose economic effects are unlikely to trickle down in a positive way for the poor but which pleases the better off, or do you go about the less glamorous process of bottom-up economic develop-ment?

It is only when we see these things from a detached, eagle's eye view that the shape and overall dynamic of things are clear. Those who move around from place to place can see the full impact of the dull sameness of the 'same place everywhere' syndrome, which is why the promise of another Guggenheim icon seems so attractive. Then the sharp dominance of global brands becomes clear, from Wal-Mart to Tesco to McDonald's to Gap, whether you are in California, Milan, Lyon, Moscow, Yokohama or Johannesburg. But locals instinctively know too that in spite of the glamour of the brands, they are a double-edged sword, endangering local distinc-tiveness. Finding an inventive route that balances the local and global is the challenge.

Which way the creativity of people is focused to make cities great places is a subtext throughout this book. It is highlighted more sharply below when we talk of the geography of desire. The question that lurks in the background is this: What if the immense energy, resources, creativity and imagination that are used to seduce us to buy more were used for different aims? Inevitably the text has a somewhat critical tone, but it is not a personal criticism of the many shopping centre managers, developers, marketers or policy-makers I meet daily through my work. They, like me and all of us, are caught in a maelstrom and a system that pushes us inexorably towards speeding up, consuming more, with greater focus on individual wants than on bigger-picture, communal needs. Many want to bend the market to more lofty aims. But to stand alone against the prevailing wind is hard.

Ordinary desire

Yet ordinary desire is a more beautifully mundane thing, a less thrusting desire, one that is softer. It is the ordinary day-to-day lived urban experience of people. It is the basic needs that count. Can I walk from where I live or work to a public space where I can just *be* rather than having to buy something? Desirable places fulfil the need for just *being*, so enabling us to experience the moment, a chance for incidental encounter, a space open for coincidence rather than having to do something specific or continuously having to consider, 'What next?' The Plaza Nueva in Bilbao fulfils this need, as does the contained Caracas town hall square or Stavanger's Sølvberget Square, where, as so often, the public library, the *Kulturhus*, is an anchor. The sensually perfect oval square Piazza dell'Anfiteatro, the shopping street Via Fillungo in Lucca or even Djemaa el Fna in Marrakech, one of the world's great squares, satisfy ordinary desire, as does idling around one of Amsterdam's many markets or even ambling along its canals. Mothers looking at their kids running around, idle chatter, old guys reading the news-paper and smoking, a stall to buy a drink or a bun, a market selling flowers and food one day, second-hand knick-knacks the next. The community centre or library, a place to browse, let a chance encounter with books or through the internet take its course, read a magazine. A city is not only a static thing consisting of its built form, but also a series of small human interactions that fill a cauldron. Ordinary culture in action.

Is the housing well designed, well built, well maintained, spacious and affordable? Does it meet the varying needs of single persons and families? Does the urban design meld the interior and exterior landscapes into an integrated whole? Does it meet the needs of privacy yet also encourage people to interact? Are uses mixed so that living, working, shopping is convenient, so that people have many reasons to cross paths and communicate in the

Source: Charles Landry

*Libraries are among the most inclusive cultural institutions ...
and Vancouver's is one of the best: note how rounded the
building is, which may account for its popularity*

simple ways that build social capital and make communities work? Can I go swimming? Is there a gym or a cinema nearby? Are services – doctors' surgeries, schools, meeting places – local? Is the rubbish cleared, does the graffiti get cleaned and do potholes get dealt with? Can I ring a council official and get someone – a human being – to answer the phone? Do I have confidence in the voluntary bodies or the businesses around me? Ordinary needs well met.

How do you get around? Does the transport system work? Is the metro clean? Does it operate frequently and without hiccup? Are suburban train lines efficient? Is the journey itself worth the experience, so you relax into the journey itself, just travelling, as you might in Hong Kong? Or is it more unpleasant, like in London, where you feel crowded in and your body tightens up and where you think of the next experience to take your mind off the present one? Does the car traffic flow through the city? Is parking available? Ordinary facilities working like clockwork.

Are there bright lights in the city core to stimulate aspiration? Are there places to hang out – special shops, cinemas, theatres, outdoor spaces for gathering, celebrating, demonstrating? Could you call your city a vibrant hub and a place of flourishing neigh-bourhoods? Is the gap between the rich and poor leavened? Are segregations reduced? Do cultures cross boundaries? Is prejudice minimal? Does it all add up? Does this stage set feel safe? Does it meld into an overall quality of life? Ordinary equality lived out in real life.

This picture exists in snatches in many of our cities without conscious planning or any new 'ism'. It is astonishing how simple this quiet desire feels, where time is slowed down and with the occa-sional burst of excitement. This is what makes café culture so appealing. Yet economic drivers go against maintaining its simplicity.

Pumping up desire

'Since 1970 the number of consumer products introduced each year has increased 16-fold'.[82] This is the inexorable dynamic that means retailing must pump up desire and push us to buy more. Yet the mall and shopping as the metaphor for a good life cannot sustain the spirit. Filling emptiness with busyness rarely works, however enticing it may appear at first sight.

In our age of consumption, we buy many things we don't need, at least not to survive biologically. Increasing purchases take on a social function, expressing sexuality, status, wealth and power. For capitalism to keep going, needs must grow and so they must be manufactured. The 'free market' propels the inexorable dynamic to get you to spend. Otherwise the system falls apart. Every sensory means is used and orchestrated to trigger the imagination: sound, smell, the look and feel, texture, colour and motion. It is enticing, it has its delights, it projects pleasure, but it is emptier than it appears. The system could not survive if it was not immensely seductive, and fashion is its name. Yet it is a hedonistic treadmill that drains our energy.

Retailing is the engine of this process, fashion the mechanism and technique, and the manufacture of dissatisfaction the result. It is a double-edged sword, twisting discontent into urges and the desire to want. The shift to compulsive consumption changes the nature of ordinary desire. All-pervasive, it changes the way we relate, so that everything feels it should be an economic transac-tion. This is a voracious desire that can never truly be satiated. You might retort, 'But you have a choice.' But when everyone around you is wanting, it is hard to go against the grain. In the past we conceived most things as necessities. Treats were less in evidence. We had less disposable money. Today many have little too, but the credit system has expanded to soak up wants, even though it might ultimately hit you and throw you back on the heap. Now treats, surprises and the new have become necessities. Think of humble spectacles or glasses, once bought once and for life. The same for your umbrella or wristwatch. Now there is Swatch and you need watches for every occasion: my dress-up watch, my dress-down watch, my sports watch, my fun watch. Think of functional Wellington boots, just there to keep out the rain for those in the countryside, by tradition usually green and on occasion black. Now they are an urban accessory. They come in bright red, translucent blue or garish yellow, and you need a different colour for every occasion. Everything is turned into a fashion item. The life span of things like clothes once stretched into the horizon. Now they quickly become disposable. Even your home. Now all too soon things are perceived to look tired and worn. This feeds the DIY craze. Even your looks are up for grabs. 'I need a makeover.' Wrinkles no longer reflect experience – they are a cosmetic nuisance. The idea of the beauty of ageing is disappearing. Everything must be young, young, young. In the end, life itself becomes a commodity, but sadly there is only one.

Out has gone the well-worn shirt fraying at the edges – chuck it instead. Or wearing a pair of shoes until you can see your experience etched into them – chuck them. We have lost the sense of small history, the little pieces of personal experience melding together into a textured life. And along the way we have lost the art of repairing and feeling a sense of trajectory and the patina of ages inscribed into things. Old clothes still look smart if worn with a quiet confidence. Instead we have to invent 'shabby chic' as a fashion type, so you have to buy new things made to look old. The production cost of making jeans look old is more than producing jeans that look new. Something always needs to make a buck, otherwise it all falls apart.

In the name of choice there is a continual roll of inventions: new breads, butters, every variation of milk, chocolates. Who thought they needed 40 varieties of candles or that 30 styles of coffee were necessary? Barry Schwartz's *The Paradox of Choice: Why More is Less* documents this and the increasing reaction to wish to simplify things well.[83] Schwartz starts with a story of trying to buy a pair of jeans in Gap and talks of the 85 brands of crackers in his local supermarket. He experiences choice overload, a condition that can make you question your decisions before you even make them, setting you up for unrealistically high expectations, where inevitably you fail and blame yourself. This can lead to decision-making paralysis. A culture of limitless choice that implies that somewhere there is perfection leads to a sense of emptiness and possible depression. We are being bred to buy and to give up on the simple pleasures of creating our own entertainment: singing, dancing, playing games, having fun and making our own things from clothes to furniture. This is a loss so strong that it has counter-reactions, which is why activities such as karaoke are so popular.

Mentally moving on before arriving

Being locked into a pattern of needing to consume forces people into a lifestyle which they cannot quite afford. And so we are dissatisfied. Continually needing makes people needy because they are permanently being shown the next thing they do not possess. The retailing dynamic unhinges the anchored self, always under threat from other causes too, as it focuses on what is missing. It changes how we perceive existence. Rather than experiencing *what is* and concentrating on the here and now and its attendant realities, it shifts focus to tomorrow and *what could be*. This means we do not appreciate the fullness of possibilities or the engagement of daily life.

Insidiously this logic has crept into other parts of our life. Everything is becoming a paid-for experience. Like a rash, the market has eviscerated much of the finer texture of urban living, the unpaid transactions that build social capital and trust. Many of these are the invisible threads upon which collaboration was built. Relationships and interactions that were once free are now set in the exchange economy; they are now a commodity. Social relations are being determined by whether you can buy. Even how you meet people is increasingly arranged, brokered and paid for. And everything has to be fast, thus the rise in speed-dating. There are fewer free activities or places to hang around, to sit around in public and not spend money. Some people, especially the elderly, now go to the doctor simply to have a chat and have human contact rather than be at home on their own.

Indeed, what does desire look like through the eyes of the elderly, the poor and those otherwise disenfranchised? They are already swept up in its maelstrom. The market has already sniffed out that there is an audience to be captured who are nurturing their savings when they could be spending them. Make them feel inadequate, make them want. Make them understand that just like a tired shop needs a design makeover or facelift, so too do older people. The poor are a harder challenge: give them a sense that everyone can be a winner, keep them wanting too. But this is a fragile balancing act, because at some point the dream has to come to fruition or else resistance might grow, endangering the whole house of cards.

Speed and slowness

The consuming logic that is never fulfilled means people want to experience more, perhaps 30 hours of experience in a 24-hour day. There is more on offer, but the same amount of time. In our desire not to waste time, we are left with even less of it. Speeding things up means substituting quantity for quality and along the way a certain depth to life is lost. Travel is faster, communicating electronically is faster. Eating has become faster – fast food is just one manifestation of this. Lunch breaks are shortening, with little time for eating, let alone digesting. Getting to know people and relationships are speeded up through speed-dating. With names like Speeddater or Hurrydate, it is possible to meet 20 people for three minutes each on an evening and decide who you want to follow up. The length of time we keep clothes has shortened. Disposability is key. The shelf-life of buildings is shorter. Room decorations can be bought off the peg and discarded with each new move. This is the throwaway city. Caterers with names like On the Run or Gourmet on the Go! ('Providing healthy, delicious meals for busy people') are proliferating.[84]

With everything speeding up, people are trying to adapt; the high visibility and immediacy of advertising messages becomes crucial and very fast instant response rates are required. People are in danger of becoming overloaded. More and more messages are trying to get through and the urban landscape is increasingly one large advertising billboard. Eye Contact, a new device, helps calculate the amount of advertising messages we receive in a day. In a large city like London we see as many images in a day as people

It's time to
arrive before
you get there.
It's time for Treo.

Email. Phone. Web.

Source: Charles Landry

Speeding up the world allows no space for reflection

saw in a lifetime in the Middle Ages, around 3500. Yet in a survey it was discovered that 99 per cent of messages are not consciously remembered.[85]

A reaction to speed is 'slowness'. Now joining the stress consultants, therapists and time-management consultants are 'slow coaches' to treat 'rushaholics':

> *At work they are management freaks, on holiday they are activity freaks, in the evening their time is jammed with social functions ... they're constantly working on their wardrobe, darting into shops buying things ... between watching a video they'll be phoning friends. A woman who was cured noted: 'I've slowed down, I live more basically and because I shop less, I want less... I've replaced quantity with quality.'*[86]

The Slow Cities movement is a reaction to speed based on ethos-driven development. Slow Cities developed out of the Slow Food movement, which started in Italy in the 1980s. Slow Food promotes the protection of local biodiversity, the right to taste through preserving local cooking and eating traditions, and highlights the folly of fast food and fast life. Slow Cities is expanding the concept to be a way of life. It emphasizes the importance of local identity through: preserving and maintaining the local natural and built environments; developing infrastructure in harmony with the natural landscape and its use; using technology to improve quality of life and the natural and urban environment; encouraging the use and production of local foodstuffs using eco-sensitive methods; supporting production based on cultural traditions in the local area; and promoting the quality of local hospitality.

The aim of the Slow Cities movement is to implement a programme of civilized harmony and activity grounded in the serenity of everyday life by bringing together communities who share this ideal. The focus is on appreciation of the seasons and cycles of nature, the cultivation and growing of local produce through slow, reflective living. Slow Cities is not opposed to progress but focuses on changes in technology and globalization as tools to make life better and easier while protecting the uniqueness of town characters. To be a member of Slow Cities and to be able to display the movement's snail logo, a city must meet a range of requirements, including increasing pedestrian access, implementing recycling and reuse policies, and introducing an ecological transport system. Working with the Slow Food network, the Slow Cities movement is spreading the word about its slow brand of community connectedness.

Trendspotting or trainspotting?

'Fashion is not just a matter of life and death, it is more... it helps define who we are.'[87] Fashion is the cause and retailing the agent of the change hysteria. Fashion has a glow, yet also a withered sadness, as what we wear is always on the cusp of going out of fashion. The industry of fashion trendspotters inexorably forges the forward path. Trendy they may seem, yet in their own way they are as obsessive as trainspotters in their raincoats and anoraks. With their ear to the ground they read the signs and symbols of changing taste and desire. They not only track change but also create it, as there are always leaders, early adopters, before the laggard majority. Being sensitive to trends helps companies stay ahead of the game, a game that is moving ever faster. Barely a decade ago there were two fashion cycles in clothing. Now there are six, requiring the frenzied change of window displays and media bombast. Car purchasing is moving down to a three-year cycle. Home makeovers, which did not exist as a concept until recently, are now on a five-year cycle. Moving house was a once-in-a-generation thing. It is now down to a seven- to ten-year cycle. Relationships are shorter and divorce no longer carries a stigma.

Consider some trends from the trendspotters – and they will have already gone by the time you read this (see box overleaf). For example, 'branded brands', 'being spaces' and 'curated consumption' are, apparently, just round the corner if not already upon us. At their core they are about individuality, not solidarity, and they seek to distinguish the individual from others, making you as the individual feel you are the most important person in the world. You become what you are through the brand and your control of it. You surround yourself with associational richness.

The shopping repertoire

We could divide the shopping world into essentials, such as food, and inessentials, like fashion accessories, but both are subject to the same forces. The competition to generate desire spills out into the landscape of cities and helps shape them. The city then becomes a desire-inducing machine. It needs to draw attention to itself for its local, national and international audiences, and a repertoire has emerged to make this happen. At its core lies shopping and culture.

Property prices are the core driver of this urban development. Retailing is the main driver of its changing shape and look. Creating the destination is the goal, generating the experience the means. The aim is to craft an experience that has rich layers that mean something. Much as people try to give products or brands depth, they still have a hollow ring as consuming, in the final analysis, has limited value. A pair of shoes is just that – a pair of shoes. Even though staying in that 'special' boutique hotel, eating refined food and going to that seductive lounge bar might be great, in the end does it give longer-term sustenance? Generating associational richness is the challenge and the city itself needs to play its part in keeping the machine speeding along. And there are alternative strategies here – one shouts louder through its sign and symbol system, another more quietly so as to project class. Yet interwoven in most strategies are arts institutions and cultural facilities as is evidenced by every single city-marketing brochure, which highlights

TRENDSPOTTING

- **Youniversal branding** At the core of all consumer trends is the new consumer, who creates his or her own playground, own comfort zone, own universe. It's the 'empowered' and 'better informed' and 'switched on' consumer combined into something profound, something we've dubbed MASTER OF THE YOUNI-VERSE. At the core is control: psychologists don't agree on much, except for the belief that human beings want to be in charge of their own destiny. Or at least have the illusion of being in charge.

- **Curated consumption** … make way for the emerging trend of CURATED CONSUMPTION: millions of consumers following and obeying the new curators of style, of taste, of eruditeness, in an ever-growing number of B2C industries (Martha and home deco-rating was really just the beginning ;-). And it's not just one way: in this uber-connected world, the new curators enjoy unprecedented access to broadcasting and publishing channels to reach their audience, from their own blogs to niche TV channels.

- **Nouveau niche** *BusinessWeek* called it The Vanishing Mass Market, *Wired Magazine* spoke of the Lost Boys and the Long Tail. Others talk about Niche Mania, Stuck in the Middle, or Commoditization Chaos. We at TRENDWATCHING.COM dubbed it NOUVEAU NICHE: the new riches will come from servicing the new niches! And while all of this may smack of wordplay, the drivers behind this trend have been building for years.

- **Branded brands** In plain English: BRANDED BRANDS means you will get a pizza from Pizzeria Uno on an American Airlines flight. And onboard perks offered by United Airlines include Starbucks Coffee, Mrs. Fields Cookies and even a McDonald's 'Friendly Skies Meal', including the ubiquitous promo-toy. Cars aren't immune either: Lexus proudly promotes their Mark Levinson audio systems. It all points to consumers on the road increasingly wanting to find the brands they trust and enjoy at home.

- **Being spaces** With face-to-face communication being rapidly replaced by email and chat, goods and services being purchased online, and big city apartments shrinking year by year, urban dwellers are trading their lonely, cramped living rooms for the real-life buzz of BEING SPACES: commercial living-room-like settings, where catering and entertainment aren't just the main attraction, but are there to facilitate small office/living room activities like watching a movie, reading a book, meeting friends and colleagues, or doing your admin.

Source: www.trendwatching.com

how vibrant their cultural scene is in terms of these institutions. For many, still, culture simply equates to museums, galleries and theatres and not a great deal else. For this reason, mobilizing these institutions remains central to cultural policy.

Architects, lighting engineers and billboard animators stand in the centre, seeking to dazzle, amaze and stun their audience. The level at which this is executed depends on the city's role in the larger world urban hierarchy. Think of the historic 'boulevards of dreams' and their resonance. They once played on a larger stage, but many now live off memories of a past heyday. They tend to attract an older audience now as their hipness has been drained out of them. The Champs-Elysées, once a place which fed desires and a synonym for Parisian chic, has lost some of its lustre and glamour, dominated as it is by airline offices and car showrooms, though it is still the site of fashion houses and expensive restaurants. Piccadilly Circus and Regent Street in London have suffered a similar fate. The Ramblas in Barcelona is perhaps overrun now by tourists, but at its best you can still watch the world and not be contained in a fence of consumption. There is Düsseldorf's Königsallee, which the locals avoid when the tourists swarm in, or Berlin's Kurfürstendamm, whose energy is waning. In the Malecon in Havana, the flow of old classic cars and the music excite, but on the down side you are aware of the clash between tourists and poor locals. The latter are tied into an oppressive relationship with the tourist; their relaxed, laid-back lifestyle contrasts with the need to hassle and compete for tourists. Ginza in Tokyo is a byword for its department stores, such as Mitsukoshi or Matsuya, into which are interspersed the trendsetting shops like Sony or the cool and sleek Apple Store. All are kept in trim by stylish new architectural insertions.

The louder response is best seen in East Asia, although Eastern Europe is also making its mark. Adverts become increasingly vertiginous – six stories high as in Hsimenting in Taipei, where to attract the young Taipei hipsters the music also pounds out so loud that the ground shakes. New York's Times Square is another instance, as is the Strip in Las Vegas. For a sheer blast of colour, action and head-spinning animated billboards, perhaps none can rival Dotonbori in Osaka, packed with people at night. It uses every latest advertising gizmo and its craziness has an outlandish beauty. To get an idea of what the future may hold in store, Japan is instructive. Its aesthetics so different from European sensibilities, it combines the stark crassness of Osaka's

Electric Town or Tokyo's Akihabara computer district with the sublime beauty of the perfectly crafted object, shop front or urban setting. They come together in Kyoto around Kiyamachi-dori and Kawaramachi-dori, calm yet exalting Zen gardens with buildings built by architects seemingly inspired by watching Star Wars on acid. Vegas looks tame and controlled by contrast. China, in frenzied growth zones like Shenzhen, is beginning to rival this new aesthetic. Cities use every trick they have to 'spectacularize' themselves: image, media and trophy buildings by 'star' architects are brought into harness.

Segmentation and area character are key, with property prices driving the design quality and focus of any area and its distinctiveness. Most large cities can be divided into high-end, mainstream, alternative and grotty. Like a Ginza or Sloane Street in London, where high-end architecture, design, image and aspiration mix, strongly fed by media attention and focused on an older, richer crowd. There are the mainstream, less rich areas like Oxford Street in London, where most day-to-day shopping takes place. Then there is the continual search for the new upcoming area. In London once Notting Hill, then Camden and now Hoxton. It is always on the move. The next will be an area that today is still relatively cheap. The very cheapness that makes an area attractive to the young and inventive is the very thing that raises prices over time. With trendspotters on the prowl, providing the media oxygen over time, the edginess is tamed and the gentrification process starts. This is both good and bad and keeping the balance of shabbiness and chic or inventiveness and convention is an immensely difficult trick. Very few places have achieved it. Amsterdam, though, is one instance. This is largely because mainstream retailers, with the profit ratios they demand and minimum size requirements for their stores, cannot impose their templates on to the city. In Amsterdam the intricate physical patterning and structure dominated by canals cannot be broken up. In addition it is extremely difficult for corporations to buy up large areas. The resulting fragmented ownership means that landlords are not always pumping up rents to their highest levels. As a consequence, the sheer number of unique shops is astonishing. Think of the Nine Streets area, the Jordaan and the myriad other small streets that offer surprise.

But when the market has unfettered leeway, the Amsterdam scenario is nearly impossible to sustain. Typically the pioneers discover an area, perhaps an old industrial site such as the

Distillery in Toronto, a set of industrial streets like Tribeca in New York or streets near a university where many young hang out, such as Deptford High Street near Goldsmith's College in London, famous for graduates like artist Damian Hurst. They try out a shop. It might succeed. The cafés come in. The word spreads. Alternatively, larger industrial structures are converted into artists' studios or incubator units for young design companies. A gallery opens; there is a cultural venue which shows fringe material; the bar there becomes popular; a restaurant opens, then another; and the gentrification process begins as it spills into the surrounding area. Gentrification remains a double-edged sword. It is an essential process through which property values rise to make it worthwhile for investors to get involved. On the other hand, it can push out those who make the gentrification process possible in the first place.

In essence, the fate of cities is determined by property prices. When a city like London or Berlin is selling its property to a global market, this will tend to price out less affluent locals. This is why we are faced with a crisis of finding accommodation for people in lower paid but crucial employment such as nurses, teachers and police, without whom a city cannot function. The gentrification of an area can spell the exclusion of key workers if left unchecked. The only solution is to contain the market and to find alternative ways of providing affordable accommodation.

A few places have tried to challenge this logic. Temple Bar in Dublin is an instance. A finely knitted pattern of streets in the heart of the city, it was once threatened with demolition to make way for a transport hub and inevitably declined with this sword of Damocles hanging over it. Many years later, when the plan was rescinded, the area's attractiveness was recognized and redevelopment was planned to make it an artistic hub. The development was controlled by a quasi-public authority which either owned or had influence on leases and tried to obviate the logic of price spirals that were inevitable given Temple Bar's central location. Its lease structures guaranteed affordable, longer-term security for the many arts organizations, such as the Irish Photography Centre, the Irish Film Institute, the Temple Bar Music Centre, the Arthouse Multimedia Centre, Temple Bar Gallery and Studio, and the Gaiety School of Acting. However, the creative vitality that these organizations represent is being threatened by over-popularity and consequent growth in tourist fodder restaurants and meat-market pubs to deal with stag and hen night parties. This has led to TASCQ (Traders in the Area Supporting the Cultural Quarter) encouraging people to stay away.

Normality is increasingly the out-of-town suburban mall associated with mid-America but now wending its way through Europe and into Asia. It is even reconfiguring shopping in India, so long a bastion of thousands of stallholders. At the moment 97 per cent of Indian retailing is by small independents. 'The malling of India', though, has become a recognized phenomenon. When it fully takes hold millions of Indians will have turned from small entrepreneurs to wage slaves. But there is resistance to the chain gang. In Singapore the food hall adjacent to Erskine Road in Chinatown has 140 independent cafés or restaurants, rather than the usual crowd of multinationals who would fit about a dozen brand names into the same space.

Asia is catching up just when the homeland of malls, America, is reconsidering their value. For many, the well-known mass brand names are enough, cosseted next to the big box retailers. Enclosed somewhere, essentially in places of no distinction in the middle of nowhere, the business of shopping can proceed conveniently with an ocean of parking spaces attached. The architecture imitates Classical or Art Deco, built to last a shopping generation that is measured in half-decades. The substance only skin deep, façades hide false ceilings and the sites can be reconfigured when required.

Making more of the night

The dream of the 24-hour city for groups of all ages has largely faded, heralding the arrival of an urban drinking environment for the young only, especially in Northern Europe. The continental European café, eating and entertainment culture, with the generations intermingling, has not happened. With cities increasingly spread out, travelling downtown is too much of an effort. The famed Mediterranean *passegiata* can only occur with vibrancy where living and shopping are close to each other. This means urban density with accommodation for single persons as well as families.

Being able to deal with the night is culturally learnt. A decade ago the symptom was dead town centres at night in places like Britain where the tradition of living together and socializing publicly in the evening had been lost. When the city began to be revalued and a shift towards an urban renaissance occurred, it led to an increased awareness of the value of public space and investment in it.[88] This occurred throughout the country, with some high quality examples, such as Brindley Place and Broad Street in Birmingham. But generally, in the early evening, city centres empty, to be reclaimed at night by mostly young drinkers, bolstered by the drinks industry with bars competing loudly for attention. The result is monocultural. Hordes of young drinkers put off other age groups. The city centres in Britain are usually very lively, yet it is an exclusionary feeling: less intergenerational, less intercultural. Children and older people hardly dare venture in. Twenty-four-hour services are limited to bars, bars, bars, restaurants, clubs and bars. Facilities to broaden the appeal of night are rare. Libraries, museums and galleries close early, some even at 5.00pm. In effect, many such places are open on weekdays when most people have no time and closed when people have time. Urban management should have a strong role in assessing the palette of possibilities in each segment of the day, as it should in the management of public space to ensure diverse use and users.

The Italians have come up with an innovative solution and are addressing the democratic deficit of the 24-hour city. At least half a dozen Italian cities now have an *Ufficio Tempi* – an Office of Time. These try to reorganize time in more flexible ways to meet new needs, especially those of women, who often juggle two timetables, work and home. The Offices of Time try to bring together transport providers, shop-owners, employers, trade unions, the police and other services to see how their efforts might mesh better to produce more flexible ways of living and working. They use time as a resource by staggering opening hours of offices, shops, schools and services to maximize time and to avoid crushes and rushes. Shops might open and close later, and police might work more in the evening when people want to see them, rather than in the morning.

The Geography of Blandness

Fifteen years ago I started to count shops on the high streets of different cities to see how many names I knew. I was disappointed. I was already beginning to recognize too many and gave up. Last year I started the counting again and idly counted the shops in

Corporate blandness, anywhereville

Cornmarket and Queen Street, the main shopping streets in
Oxford, one of Britain's most distinctive cities. I knew the names of
85 out of 94. I experienced a lurching feeling of dullness. In those
15 years, the world of retailing in Britain has changed dramatically,
with the march of malls and global brands sucking the life out of
ordinary high streets. I have travelled too by car, criss-crossing the
suburbs and outer entrances of cities from Europe to North
America, Australia and elsewhere: always the same picture, always
the same names. Thought experiments kept coming into my mind.
What if you lined up all the 30,000 McDonald's in the world next
to each other – how long would the McDonald's road strip be? Six
hundred kilometres or so? And then add the 25,000 Subways,
11,000 Burger Kings, 11,000 KFCs, 6800 Wendy's and 6500 Taco
Bells? Hey, if we line up the ten top fast-food chains, they will
stretch half the 4504 kilometres from New York to Los Angeles. A
chilling thought. And even Starbucks has over 11,000 outlets with
joint ventures. Then I went though the same exercise with other
shops, like Gap, which has 3050 outlets, before a headache set in
and I stopped. This is the geography of blandness, and the blanding processes are worldwide, as witnessed by counter-activities such
as the 'Keep Louisville Weird' campaign, which, picked up on from

WEIRD = 'OF STRANGE OR EXTRAORDINARY CHARACTER'

Keep Louisville Weird is a grassroots public awareness campaign, recently and quietly begun by a small but growing coalition of independent Louisville business owners who are concerned with the spreading homogenization of our hometown. We're concerned that the proliferation of chain stores and restaurants in Louisville is not only driving the independent business owner out of business, but is also robbing the city of much of its unique charm. While we don't discount the need for the Wal-Marts of the world, we're troubled by the current civic notion that excitement for our town should come from the courting, establishment and promotion of chain stores and restaurants that can be found in many other cities across America.[89]

Suddenly large billboards started dotting parts of Louisville with a striking black and white design and with the simple message 'Keep Louisville Weird'... and then there were T-shirts ... and bus cards ... and stickers. No one knew where they had come from. And the story behind the 'Keep Louisville Weird' motto did not come out until almost a year later. By then, the media were raring to cover it.

The billboards were placed by an informal coalition of independent Louisville businesses – a protest against 'Starbucksification', sparked by the sale of Hawley-Cooke, Louisville's largest independent bookstore, to Borders in August 2003. They borrowed the 'Keep My Town Weird' idea from a similar slogan on car bumpers in Austin: 'Collaborative fission of coordinated individualism'.

bumper stickers from Austin, has been followed by others like 'Keep Portland Weird'.

The march of the mall

Regional malls initially started without too much of a threat to diversity. They had foundation stores to 'anchor' an end of the mall, typically then a department store. In between were several specialty shops, often smaller local traders relocating from older, declining shopping areas. But to ensure the highest possible rent, mall operators preferred leasing to stores with proven track records, especially those with marketing success in malls. Few small, local stores could match the track records of national specialty retailers, chains of stores specializing in a single product niche but operating internationally, such as Gap, Williams-Sonoma (cooking supplies), Dorothy Perkins and Benetton. As the market became saturated with malls, specialty retailers thrived even when malling declined.

Malls began homogenizing by the early 1990s. They now break down into three broad categories, driven by class and income. 'A' malls cater to upper- and upper-middle-class shoppers. In the US they include department stores, such as Neiman Marcus, Saks Fifth Avenue and Bloomingdale's; exclusive national specialty clothing retailers like Ralph Lauren and Kenneth Cole; household goods stores like Pottery Barn and Crate & Barrel; and national niche stores that appeal to broader audiences, such as Gap. 'B' malls are targeted more at middle- and partly upper-middle-class shoppers. Their department stores have large selections, but not as large or as exclusive as those in 'A' malls. While the mix of specialty shops in 'B' malls is similar to those in 'A' malls, retailers like Bulgari, Yves Saint Laurent and Tiffany & Co. would not locate in 'B' malls. Others, such as Banana Republic, offer reduced selections of merchandise. 'C' malls cater to middle- and lower-middle-class shoppers. Their department stores only target people with lower incomes. Specialty retailers that seek to attract wealthier shoppers, such as J. Crew or Abercrombie & Fitch, will not locate stores in 'C' malls.

This retail mix renting strategy significantly reduced risks for mall operators but has created a monotonous shopping experience for consumers, who want a more varied choice. Visitors increasingly feel the convenience of one-stop, climate-controlled shopping in regional malls is counter-balanced by the inconveniences of parking, ever-expanding buildings and limited choice heavily focused on national speciality retail stores.

Two approaches are being offered as an alternative to regional malls. The first is the 'big box' shopping centre, which is essentially a strip mall that contains several very large stores. There, outlets are 10–20 times the size of the speciality mall store. Shoppers park their cars in parking lots directly in front of the store. Depending on where you are you see Best Buy, Home Depot, Currys, Halfords or Office Depot. The second is to reinvent the old high street: the 'main street mall', combining big box and smaller shops, designed

Source: Charles Landry

*A good secondary shopping street in Cork, Ireland –
the kind that is disappearing very rapidly*

to resemble the fantasy of a main street in a small American community at the turn of the 20th century. The storefronts in main street malls, like those of early malls, face a pedestrian walkway. Parking is tucked inconspicuously behind the building.[90]

The bland processes of malling, shedding and big boxing have reconfigured cities dramatically. They tore older cities apart by inserting malls inside their cores, losing the street in the process and breaking up community patterns, rupturing the historic urban fabric. Placement on the edge of town or out of town drains the city of its lifeblood – a process well documented. It has led to the decline of local shopping and the attendant network of relationships. It has made facilities like libraries and other services feel out of place, because they are now separated from shopping.[91] It has helped the process by which chains have become ever dominating, providing the larger templates they require. Yet what irony! Back in 1956, when the first mall was opened in Minnesota (Southdale Mall in Edina, a suburb of Minneapolis), the father of the enclosed mall, Victor Gruen, stated that the mall was the way to replicate community by providing social interaction and recreation in pedestrian-friendly environments by incorporating civic and educa-

---

RECREATING THE PAST FOR THE FUTURE

As much as malls and shopping centers have morphed in the past few years, even more changes are coming. The retail cycle is shrinking, change is accelerating and store sizes and formats are in flux. There will be some stunning new designs and lots of white-hot technology, but the biggest changes will be less obvious: redesigned malls with different kinds of anchors and different tenant mixes, and lots more space for non-retail uses. Everywhere, there will be a new focus on convenience, including, perhaps, daycare facilities and a place to check your coat.

No one can say for certain what the world of 2013 will look like, and interviews with industry insiders produce some predictable predictions. Developers with a heavy focus on enclosed malls say they'll remain the big dogs; those who've invested deeply in lifestyle and power centers think that they'll be on top, and that a lot of the older enclosed malls will be long gone.

Get beyond those disagreements, though, and a common vision emerges. The retail center of the future – whether it is enclosed or open-air, big or small, themed or general – will be designed to resemble a community, not just a place to shop. That means environments that place as much emphasis on recreation (everything from skate parks to jogging paths to entertainment complexes) as they do on consumption. The developments under way in 2003, as well as various remalling/demalling, already point to a future in which retail blends with other functions.

Source: excerpted from 'The Future' by Charles Hazlett, published on the *Retail Traffic* website, 1 May 2003, http://retailtrafficmag.com/mag/retail_future/index.html

---

tional facilities. It filled rather than created a void, he said. What irony again to note that the latest retail trend is to recreate community precisely along the lines of that which retailing took apart in the first place, often on the edge of town. The developers made money taking things apart and now are making it again putting it back together. Yet what was lost in the process? The walkable place where living, working and having fun are in close proximity, with doctors and dentists nearby, schools accessible, a park... Precisely what they are now recreating.

For the aspiring city that wants to project an edge, an imagination or to play on a world stage, the simplistic, low-textured mall is not enough. Think of Harajuku in Tokyo. The chains are present on the traditional gridded streets. Yet whereas most American teenagers follow the dictates of fashion provided by stores like Gap, Urban Outfitters, Hot Topic or any large national or international chain, many teenagers in Harajuku set the trends that are then taken up by the fashion industry. They are not the followers of trends dictated from the top of the fashion food chain. Like peacocks showing their feathers, teens go through an amazing ritual of preening, creating a visual feast, claiming the area as their own along the way. Garish colours shout, subverting traditional Japanese styles and borrowing from Western ones. They create elaborate shapes and hairstyles and, with their powdered faces, they are punky and rebellious. They twist perceptions and warp them into a strong tension of ritualized behaviour and controlled wildness.

Think of restaurant brands. Whether upscale or run-of-the-mill, they do not register on the 'desirometer'. Thirty thousand McDonald's or 11,500 Burger Kings do not get the blood racing. Consider instead Zurich's Blinde Kuh (Blind Cow), set up in 2000, which has taken the city by storm. (Similar ventures have been set up in Paris and London.[92]) This combines gastronomy with a social purpose. These are restaurants where you can't see – you eat in total darkness – and the waiters are blind. Only the manager and the receptionist are sighted. Blinde Kuh is owned by a charity, Blindlight, set up by Jorge Spielmann, a blind clergyman. The meal creates a bonding experience between diners and makes sighted people focus on their senses afresh, which many find profound. For blind diners it can be liberating and those going blind can show their partners what life may be like.

The death of diversity and ordinary distinctiveness

Once upon a time, not so long ago, people used to shop on foot in their local high street. They bought individual products from different retailers: screws from the hardware store, bread from the baker, meat from the butcher, fruit and veg from the greengrocer. This process developed an invisible web of community. Those days are gone. Instead, supermarkets reign supreme and they are aggressively expanding their offer of non-food goods.[93] The one-stop shop only appears beneficial, however, because we think we are time-pressured and convenience-driven. The high streets, the malls and big box centres all look similar and to create distinctiveness they need to spice up the bland with 'total experiences'. There are gains and losses in this process.

We have lost the option of shopping at small, local, specialist shops and building relationships with owners. The link with supermarkets check-out staff is minimal. Fifty years ago in Britain, independents made up half of the market; now the figure is below 15 per cent. Between 1997 and 2002, 13,000 specialized shops – bookshops, hardware stores, butcher's, baker's, fishmonger's, chemist's, multipurpose corner shops, newsagent's, clothes shops, whatever specialism you care to think of – were lost. In 2004 alone, 2157 independents were lost. Overall that is nearly 50 per week. Add to this the branches of post offices, banks and building societies and the pubs and the figure doubles. Based on current trends, 33 per cent of local outlets will have shut between 1990 and 2010. These deep changes sound the death knell for local economies, and it is happening everywhere. The decline in neighbourhood shops and services breaks up the social fabric on the way and replaces it with large-scale, industrialized, corporate landscapes and relationships. Left behind are deserts where communities no longer have easy access to local shops and services; you get an increasing sense of multiplying ghost towns.[94] The result is a bland, imitative shopping landscape of multiple retailers, fast-food chains and global fashion outlets. And the decline of local shops forces many to travel greater distances to do their shopping, even in the largest cities.

This process has insidious downstream side effects, affecting the system as a whole. As smaller shops close, the number of suppliers to small shops dwindles, leading to a Catch 22 situation. Without local suppliers, local retailers suffer; and when local retailers close, suppliers suffer as they become increasingly reliant on a handful of supermarket purchasers. These in turn hold them in a vice-like grip. Between 1997 and 2002, the number of UK farm workers fell by 100,000 as supply chains globalized. Supermarket chains are not interested in the 'real' economy and real costs of food miles. And the popularity of the new 'local' stores emerging under the big supermarket brand banners presents yet another threat to independent stores.[95] Supermarkets and malls eviscerate the city.

A 2005 report by the All-Party Parliamentary Group for Small Shops stated, 'Small and independent shops may vanish from the UK's high streets by as early as 2015 ... The erosion of small shops is viewed as the erosion of the social glue that binds communities together.'[96] The British Retail Consortium responded that the group was 'trying to turn the clock back'. And a Tesco spokesperson, seemingly quoting Britain's largest retailer's PR manual, delivered the rather ignorant statement, 'The consumer is the best regulator and there is room in a thriving market for anyone who satisfies customers.' How very ironic, then, that the US trade magazine *Retail Traffic*'s issue on future trends in retailing in May 2003 cited recreating a sense of community as the key trend for the next decade. The retailing logic that tore quite resilient communities apart is now trying to put them together again in its own image and on its own terms.

Governments can only deal with wider issues of social exclusion, disadvantage and poverty if they understand that an economic system seen as 'natural' favours the large, the distant and the uniform. It damages diversity, choice, local economies and communities. Conversely, 'relocalizing' the economy empowers communities. It requires courage and tenacity to resist the lobbying capacity and media-savviness of the large retailing giants and to address the pressures of the wider economic forces head-on to create a balance between local and global economies. This requires understanding real economic value flows or local transaction analysis and distinguishing it from surface value.[97] And this in turn means redefining what we understand and measure as progress and finding ways to make the invisible value of things – social, cultural and environmental values – visible.

The New Economics Foundation proposes measures to restore local communities and shopping cultures. These include:

- **Local Communities Sustainability Bills.** Based on a bottom-up philosophy, these bills would create a coherent framework for pro-local policies by giving local authorities, communities and citizens a powerful voice in planning their future to guarantee dynamic and environmentally sustainable local economies. In 2003 such a proposed bill got the support of 33 per cent of British MPs. The goal is a 'realignment of power between the forces driving ghost and clone towns and those seeking to build more healthy, vibrant and sustainable local economies'.
- **Local competition policy.** In France, the Royer and Raffarin laws have limited the development of new supermarkets over the past few years, requiring special approval for any proposed new retail store bigger than 300m². This has guaranteed the

BLANDNESS AND
CITY IDENTITY

Italy and France have so far been able to resist the arguments, blandishments and pressures towards blandification coming from the large chains in the name of efficiency and progress. Many of their so-called restrictive planning guidelines are precisely those that are securing diversity and resisting what the French call '*la Londonization*'.

Paris approved a Local Urbanism Plan in 2005 which seeks to encourage small shops and key workers to stay in the city. It seeks to sustain the economic, social and cultural ecology of Paris, not in a nostalgic way but to strengthen locality and diversity. Central Paris, with just over 2 million residents, is far livelier because it has a dense and varied network of shops and people. It wants to sustain the social balance that makes Paris what it is and not have a place with the rich on one side and the poor on the other.

It seeks to achieve this goal by influencing the market through regulation and incentives. To nurture *la mixité sociale*, a requirement for developers is to set aside 25 per cent of any project spanning more than 1000m^2 for social housing apartments in districts where there is little at present. The majority of these will be reserved for key workers, such as teachers, nurses, council employees and shopkeepers, who are rapidly being driven out of a city where many residents rent their homes, endangering the social fabric.

To enhance a vibrant local retail sector on the streets of Paris and to sustain its distinctive food culture, half the 71,000 shops in Paris have restrictions placed on them to prevent inappropriate change of use when the shopkeeper either sells up or retires. This means that a small food shop would have to remain a food shop, and it would prevent, for example, a string of mobile phone chain shops replacing butchers, bakers or greengrocers. The move follows studies showing that the number of delicatessens has fallen by 42.8 per cent in the past decade, with butchers falling by 27.2 per cent, fishmongers by 26 per cent and bakers by 16.2 per cent. At the same time, the number of mobile telephone shops has risen by 350 per cent, fast-food restaurants by 310 per cent and gymnasiums by 190 per cent. Other measures in the plan include a requirement for developers to set aside 2 per cent of any new building for residents' bicycles and pushchairs. On the other hand it will reduce the number of parking spaces they are required to create.[98]

diversity of French shopping. Poland has also enacted similar versions of this law.

- **Using planning law to protect locally owned stores.** Planning gain agreements, such as Section 106 in Britain, which usually grant planning permits to social housing, should extend to include locally owned stores.
- **Introducing a retail takeover moratorium and limit market share to 10 per cent.** Tesco in Britain, for example, currently has a market share of over 30 per cent; the next three each have over 10 per cent.
- **Extending local tax relief to independents,** such as newsagents, and food, beverage and tobacco retailers, particularly those in villages, town centres and deprived urban neighbourhoods.
- **Undertaking local money flow analyses.** Local authorities, planning agencies, regeneration bodies and regional development agencies need to monitor local money flows to help guide local retail development.
- **Setting requirements for economic and community impact studies.**
- **Holding local referenda on major developments** that affect the identity of localities. Some issues, such as local identity, are so important that the ordinary democratic process is not enough.[99]

The curse of convenience

The blanding process needs to be counteracted by creating the lure of excitement and massive choice. A brief excursion into the world of supermarkets reveals that in Britain, the big four control nearly 75 per cent of food retailing, a frightening figure. Tesco has 30.6 per cent, Asda (Wal-Mart) 16.6 per cent, Sainsbury's 16.3 per cent and Morrison's 11.1 per cent.[100] They have drained the life out of the high street and cleansed it of diversity. The supermarket model is also space eating and they have wrenched space away from the edge of town and out of town.

Looking at their activities through a broader food miles and sustainability perspective, they are far less efficient than they make out. They have sidled into the imagination of the public as the one-stop destination for your every need. They have projected themselves as the only way. They are not stupid and they have a wealth of expertise and resources at their fingertips to lobby, to change minds and to get their way. And when the going gets tough, they adapt, chameleon-like, and pretend to be local in their desire to please. Many fund local initiatives, as long they can get on with business as usual. In sum, they pull the wool over our eyes so we do not understand the underlying dynamics of their operations and their impact on real life. These guys are professionals, exert immense power and are in it for the long haul.

Few other shops swallow such a huge chunk of our net income as supermarkets do. Tesco, for example, takes £1 in every £8 pounds spent in British shops. Do we get the value we are promised? Comparing the big chains and local, independent shops on the high street, the result is surprising. *Guardian* journalist Sarah Marks conducted an experiment over two weeks. In the first week, she spent £105.65 at Sainsbury's. In week two, a total of £105.20 at local shops was spent on the same groceries. A difference of 45p is admittedly not an enormous amount and she had to walk around more.

Nevertheless, local retailers suffer because there is a perception that the big four are cheaper and because they tell us they are 'good value'. But they rely on people only knowing the cost of a small number of goods, referred to as known value items (KVIs). These are items that supermarkets price check against their supermarket and independent competitors and keep as low as possible to attract custom. Other items can be much more expensive. Bananas are one KVI and the local market cannot match the price. But other fruit, like seedless white grapes, can be twice as expensive in the supermarkets. There is a 'hierarchy of value', with extra cheap ranges, everyday prices and premium brands. Basic sliced white bread cost Sarah Marks just 19p, but its country style with rye loaf was eight times more expensive at £1.49. Overall, chemist and grocery items in the supermarket were cheaper by 11 per cent and 28 per cent respectively, but fruit and veg, meat and fish were not.[101] What are the gains and losses in shopping in different ways? In one you support the local economy and in the other the corporatized economy with global supply chains.

Supermarkets have maintained their power because of their convenience and seductive tricks like pumping out smells near the bread counters. But how else? The planning system is weak in practically all countries and favours multiple retailers over independent stores. In Britain, in contrast to France, the government's Planning Policy Statement 6 (PPS6) is failing to prevent out-of-town development, possibly as a result of supermarkets lobbying central government. Yet PPS6 forms the only formal defence that local authorities have against retail development that may negatively impact on the community. On the one hand the policy states it is 'facilitating and promoting sustainable and inclusive patterns of development, including the creation of vital and viable town centres'. On the other, about 60 per cent of development still takes place out of town, with a rising percentage in edge-of-town locations. PPS6 also states, 'Larger stores may deliver benefits for consumers and local planning authorities should seek to make provision for them in this context. In such cases, local planning authorities should seek to identify, designate and assemble larger sites adjoining the primary shopping area (i.e. in edge-of-centre locations).'[102] But local authorities have no ultimate control. Supermarkets are beginning to have more power than local councils, as local decisions are being overturned on appeal by higher authorities. Councils are also influenced by the very high costs of appeal and are reluctant to lose. As one councillor, also a shop-owner, noted:

> *Tesco has hit the town really badly. My typical daily turnover went down 50 per cent the day it opened... They are too big and powerful for us. If we try and deny them, they will appeal, and we cannot afford to fight a planning appeal and lose. If they won costs, it could bankrupt us.*[103]

This is the result of supermarket lobbying and leveraging planning gain whereby a developer agrees with a planning authority to pay for community facilities in return for planning approval. Supermarkets run lobbying and public relations campaigns focused on local authorities and communities respectively in order to increase the likelihood that planning applications for their stores and the stores themselves, once constructed, will be accepted.

The focus on out-of-town and edge-of-town development reduces creativity because it is geared towards branded, global chains. A feeling of public space may be propagated but in reality it is privately owned space that is tightly controlled to foster a consuming environment. There is little or no room for individual participation and invention. One could imagine food chains and other stores rethinking their service delivery so that people can use city centres without worrying too much about carrying things about. Internet grocery shopping with home delivery is one development but as are local pick-up points where shoppers collect their shopping without worrying about being at home at a certain time. Such delivery innovations lessen the imperative of supermarkets to locate on the edge of town.

Clearly some chains have better track records than others, such as Waitrose in Britain, which has a good reputation for quality and is owned by its employees and not shareholders. As one would expect, this produces a high level of commitment among employees and a far stronger commitment to locality. In contrast are Wal-Mart and Tesco.

Wal-Mart is the world's largest retailer, with more than 3000 stores in the US and almost 1300 international operations, such as Asda in Britain. It is also the world's largest corporation. It employs 1.4 million workers worldwide and with over a million in the US it is the largest private employer there. More than half of Wal-Mart's US employees leave the company each year. They earn an average hourly wage of US$11.00 for non-management positions, with no defined benefit pension and inadequate healthcare. Wal-Mart was sued 4851 times in 2000 – or about once every two hours, every day of the year. Wal-Mart lawyers list about 9400 open cases.[104] They pay below poverty-level wages. At 34 hours per week (full-time at Wal-Mart), a person makes US$19,000 per year, well below the poverty level for a family of four. Six hundred and sixty thousand of its employees are without company-provided health insurance, forcing workers to seek taxpayer-funded public assistance. A US congressional study found that Wal-Mart costs the American taxpayer up to US$2.5 billion in public assistance to subsidize its US$10 billion in profits. But the going may be getting tougher. Wal-Mart won city council approval in May 2004 to build its first store in Chicago after months of delay and intense lobbying by the chain's foes and supporters. After a raucous debate, the council voted 32 to 15 to allow Wal-Mart to construct a 150,000-square-foot store in a poor, largely black and Hispanic neighbourhood on the city's West Side. In a second vote, however, the council rejected a huge store that Wal-Mart wanted to build in a racially diverse, largely middle-class South Side neighbourhood.[105] In June 2005 Vancouver city council rejected (by eight votes to three) Wal-Mart's bid to build its first store in the city, a big-box outlet on Southeast Marine Drive, this in spite of the green design that Wal-Mart put forward after criticisms of its environmental practices. As councillor Peter Ladner noted, 'There was a real "undercurrent" that wasn't officially part of the council's debate about Wal-Mart's labour practices, its sourcing practices, the satanic nature of giant multinational corporations.'[106]

In 2005 producer/director Robert Greenwald made an emblematic film called *Wal-Mart: The High Price of Low Cost*, which took the viewer on an extraordinary journey that could change the way people think, feel and shop.[107] It tracked the conditions of workers at Wal-Mart, the company's intimidation of employees, its power over supply chains and the culture of fear it induces. It allowed these people to tell their story. The film really came alive when it utilized footage of deserted towns and main streets all across America, many of which had been affected by Wal-Mart and other big-box stores moving in and causing destruction. It was released through an alternative distribution network via thousands of house parties.[108]

Similarly, there is a growing movement of people in towns and cities across Britain who believe Tesco and other big superstores threaten to destroy their communities and reduce choice. Increasingly, local people are joining together to fight new supermarket developments that they believe pose a grave threat to the health of their local economies and communities. 'Tesco has driven down the supply price of meat, vegetables, everything, because they have such a huge share of the market. It's a monopoly position... they can simply go and find someone else who will supply them at the price they want.'[109] The Tescopoly Alliance documents these campaigns. Britain is renowned for its apple varieties and quality, yet surveys by Friends of the Earth show that, at the height of the British apple season, over 50 per cent of Tesco's apples are imported and that supermarkets reject perfectly good British fruit for no good reason. Tesco says it has 7000 regional (i.e. Welsh, Scottish, Irish and English) lines on sale and many promotions related to regional produce. Yet this figure is less than 20 per cent of the total of 40,000 Tesco lines and many of these 'regional' products are sold throughout Britain so are simply British produce.[110]

Many people choose locally grown produce because of the associated environmental and social benefits. Yet ethics are increasingly marketed as a consumer choice rather than a corporate standard. Fairness and justice in trading, for example, are niched as fair-trade-labelled speciality products and not mainstreamed into business practice as of late 2005. Tesco sells only 91 fair trade product lines, a tiny amount representing only 0.2 per cent of its lines. In

November 2004 no more than 4.5 per cent of Tesco's sales of bananas were fairly traded.[111]

Tesco, like other major chains, claims to create more jobs, but the figures do not add up. In 2004 small grocery shops in the UK had a turnover of around £21 billion and employed more than 500,000[112] while Tesco, with a £29 billion turnover, employed just 250,000 people.[113] As retail chains grow, overall jobs are lost. This might be more efficient in narrow terms, but not when taking into account downstream impacts. Furthermore, the buying power of the big chains is considered to be distorting competition to a worrying degree.[114] Londis, the national corner shop brand, has admitted that it is cheaper to buy brands from Tesco and resell them than to get them from its wholesalers.[115] Tesco may claim to be a 'magnet for market towns, keeping people shopping locally',[116] but the reality is that local shops close wherever Tesco goes, from Dumfries in the north to Penzance in the south. 'The new Tesco in Dumfries now sells chart music cheaper than me, so people now only come to me for the rare stuff and the staple 35 per cent of my income from the chart music has disappeared,' says an independent record retailer.[117] The idea that regeneration can be driven by major chains needs close and sophisticated examination and appropriate and robust policy. Friends of the Earth suggest:

- a much stricter code of practice to ensure suppliers along the whole chain are treated fairly and which covers sustainability, labour and health standards;
- a supermarket watchdog to ensure that the grocery market is operating in the interests of consumers, farmers and small retailers;
- enlargement of competition policy to address impacts on suppliers (not just consumers) to prevent misuse of buying power; and
- a market study by competition authorities to examine the wider effects on society of the over-concentrated retail sector with a view to presenting policies to address market share.[118]

Shedland

You come across iconic and representational buildings, new and old, more often as you drive to the core of the city. Yet the city is more than icons. Office parks, industrial estates, housing quarters rich and poor frame the overall urban experience. Perhaps the most dispiriting areas are shedland. This is the visual experience of most places when you navigate the ring roads and dual carriageways that feed into the city: cheap, windowless, large buildings of steel frames, corrugated iron and pre-cast slabs. They are distribution hubs or light industrial sites. Their blandness neutralizes the surrounding landscape. They are lifeless. Occasionally a garish logo is the only visual relief. Built with a short shelf-life in mind, perhaps 10 or 20 years, they are part of the throwaway, disposable city. Can you imagine the artist of the mid-21st century suddenly deciding to move into these as the new live/work space as they have in the solid brick buildings of the industrial age? What new areas can artists discover when all the industrial buildings have been used up?